Lucy Cecil White Lillie

The Story of Music and Musicians for Young Readers

Lucy Cecil White Lillie

The Story of Music and Musicians for Young Readers

ISBN/EAN: 9783337084448

Printed in Europe, USA, Canada, Australia, Japan

Cover: Foto ©Thomas Meinert / pixelio.de

More available books at **www.hansebooks.com**

THE STORY
OF
MUSIC AND MUSICIANS
FOR
YOUNG READERS

BY

LUCY C. LILLIE
AUTHOR OF
"THE STORY OF ENGLISH LITERATURE FROM CHAUCER TO COWPER"
"PRUDENCE" "MILDRED'S BARGAIN" "NAN" ETC.

𝔈𝔩𝔩𝔲𝔰𝔱𝔯𝔞𝔱𝔢𝔡

NEW YORK
HARPER & BROTHERS, FRANKLIN SQUARE

HARPER'S YOUNG PEOPLE SERIES.

Illustrated. Post 8vo, Cloth, Ornamental, $1 25 per vol.

LATEST ISSUES:

RAFTMATES. A Story of the Great River. By KIRK MUNROE.
CANOEMATES. A Story of the Florida Reefs and Everglades. By KIRK MUNROE.
CAMPMATES. A Story of the Plains. By KIRK MUNROE.
DORYMATES. A Tale of the Fishing Banks. By KIRK MUNROE.
THE MYSTERY OF ABEL FOREFINGER. By WILLIAM DRYSDALE.
THE MATE OF THE "MARY ANN." By SOPHIE SWETT.
FLYING HILL FARM. By SOPHIE SWETT.
YOUNG LUCRETIA, and Other Stories. By MARY E. WILKINS.
THE MIDNIGHT WARNING, and Other Stories. By EDWARD H. HOUSE.
THE MOON PRINCE, and Other Nabobs. By RICHARD KENDALL MUNKITTRICK.
DIEGO PINZON. By JOHN RUSSELL CORYELL.
PHIL AND THE BABY, AND FALSE WITNESS. Two Stories. By LUCY C. LILLIE.
A BOY'S TOWN. Described for HARPER'S YOUNG PEOPLE. By W. D. HOWELLS.

PUBLISHED BY HARPER & BROTHERS, NEW YORK.

☞ *The above works are for sale by all booksellers, or will be sent by the publishers, postage prepaid, to any part of the United States, Canada, or Mexico, on receipt of the price.*

Copyright, 1886, by HARPER & BROTHERS.

Dedicated
TO
MY DEAR SISTER

JANET EDMONDSON WALKER

IN REMEMBRANCE OF MANY MUSICAL ASSOCIATIONS

AT HOME AND ABROAD

PREFACE.

The only necessity for a preface to this little book is to explain that the work is not designed to take the place of text-books, works on harmony or thorough-bass, or those interesting lives of the great musicians which competent writers have given to us. Its object is only to interest young students in music in the technique of their art, and in the associations amid which great masters have worked. Only such rules of harmony are given as have a direct bearing upon the subject or composition under discussion, and these I have presented, after comparing them with standard authorities, in as simple a fashion as possible, relying upon any reader who is a thoughtful student progressing to technical study under a scientific instructor. Meanwhile some impetus and enthusiasm may be added, from reading this simple story of an art which all nations are in some fashion developing to-day, and which had its origin in an age that gave a significance to the victor crown of bay-leaves and laurel.

CONTENTS.

CHAPTER I.
The Piano-forte.—Its History.—Clavichord, Virginal, and Spinet.—Anecdote of Queen Elizabeth.—An Old Harpsichord.—Piano-forte playing in the Time of Bach, Mozart, and Beethoven .... Page 13

CHAPTER II.
Musical Standards Yesterday and To-day.—How to Enjoy the Story of any Art. — A Harmony Class. — A Fascinating Story. —Early Notation.—A Musical Note-book.................................... 30

CHAPTER III.
How to Feel about Study.—First Steps.—The Key-board.—The Family of Notes.—Staff.—Degrees.—Intervals.—How to Understand the First Rules of Harmony.—Suggestions for Note-book.................. 46

CHAPTER IV.
John Sebastian Bach.—His Early Childhood.—The *Gavotte.*—Its Origin.—A Court Dance.—The Fugue.—Explanation of this Form of Composition.—Passion Music.—Anecdote of the Basques.—How Mendelssohn revived Bach's Passion Music............................ 53

CHAPTER V.
Rhythm and Time.—Bach's Developments.—A Simple Explanation.—Keys and their Families.—A Bach Fugue.—Minor Scales.—Modula-

tions.—Accidentals.—A few Words about Signatures.—Why Handel and his Contemporaries discarded the lowest Note of the Signature..Page 69

CHAPTER VI.

George Frederick Handel. — An English Country-house. — A Young Lady's Impressions of the great Composer in 1711.—"Tweedledum and Tweedledee."—"Rinaldo" and other Operas.—A Friendly Coterie.—"The Harmonious Blacksmith."—"Mr. Handel" in Dublin.— Mr. Dubourg.—The First Performance of the "Messiah."—Last Days. —Definition and History of the Oratorio........................79

CHAPTER VII.

The Story of the Opera.—Count Vernio and his Friends.—A Musical Centre in Florence.—The First Opera.—Instruments used.—Allesandro Scarlatti.—Stradella.—The Size of the Opera in England.—Henry Purcell and the Westminster Boys.— An Old Picture.— Gluck and Marie Antoinette.—Gluck's Boyhood.—Fashion and Art.—Gluck determined to Reform the Spirit of the Opera.—Classical Music, and how to Define it..94

CHAPTER VIII.

"Papa Haydn."—What came of a Frolic.—The Wig-maker's Household.—The Wandering Minstrels.—"Whose Music is that?"—Symphonies.—What they are.—Haydn's Last Hours................114

CHAPTER IX.

The Story of the Sonata.—Suites and Madrigals.—Corelli's Work.—Anecdote of Handel in Rome.—"C Major."—The Movements of the Sonata Explained and Defined.—Old Dances and Dance Tunes.—What the Minstrels and Soldiers of the Sixteenth Century Introduced.—Minuets. — Scherzos..124

CHAPTER X.

Wolfgang Amadeus Mozart.—"Master and Miss Mozart, Prodigies of Nature."—A Concert in the London of 1765.—"Nannerl."—The Chil-

Contents.

dren's Presents.—Home Discipline.—The House in Chelsea.—Playing and Composing.—The First Symphony.—An Old Letter.—Duets a Novelty.—In Italy.—The First Opera.—An Important Visit.—The Weber Family.—A Heartless Coquette.—Constanza.—"The Magic Flute."—Last Days..................................Page 134

CHAPTER XI.

Ecclesiastical Music.—Early Writers.—Palestrina and the Council of Trent.—An Important Decision.—The Reform.—Mass Music of Various Composers...150

CHAPTER XII.

Ludwig von Beethoven.—Boyhood and First Studies.—At the Princess Lichnowsky's.—Cold Water and Compositions.—An Amusing Anecdote.—Sad Years.—"Adelaide."—Blind!—Last Days............164

CHAPTER XIII.

Beethoven and the Concerto.—Explanation of this Form of Composition. —Viadana.—Difference between Composers' Methods.—Cadenzas, and what they mean..173

CHAPTER XIV.

Carl Maria von Weber.—Story of his Life.—A Baby Prodigy.—Anecdote of his Life at the Court of Wurtemberg.—"Der Freischütz."—In London with Moscheles.—A Last Visit.—Asleep.—Overtures and their Origin.—Structure.—Weber's Work.—Mendelssohn's Use of the Term.—Overtures of English Composers......................177

CHAPTER XV.

The Orchestra of Yesterday and To-day.—Its Origin.—Distinction between Orchestras and Bands.—A Wedding Celebration in the Sixteenth Century.—Duc de Joyeuse.—Lutes and Viols.—First Orchestra on Record.—Italian Developments.—Scarlatti's Obligato.—One Hundred Years of Progress.—List of Instruments.—Chamber Music. —A Conductor's Responsibility.—First Use of the Baton.—Mendelssohn's Facility in remembering Work.—An old Sketch-book.....188

CHAPTER XVI.

Felix Mendelssohn-Bartholdy.—Work and Play.—The Juvenile Orchestra.—A Pretty Picture.—Fanny Mendelssohn.—A Famous Journey.—A Letter from Goethe's House.—Moscheles in Berlin.—A Memorable Evening.—The E-flat Concerto.—Work and Recreation.—Fanny's Marriage.—In London and at Birmingham.—With the Moscheleses.—A Happy Marriage.—Founding the Conservatory of Leipsic.—Fanny's Sudden Death.—The "Elijah."—"And behold, the Lord passed by."—Last Days...Page 197

CHAPTER XVII.

A Trio: Chopin, Schubert, and Schumann.—Chopin in Paris.—Anecdote of a Memorable Visit.—Flowers and Nocturnes.—A Brief Story.—Schubert's Life.—Teaching School and Composing.—One Stormy Afternoon.—"The Erl King."—Beethoven's Friendship.—Last Days.—Robert Schumann.—A Brilliant Genius.—Little Clara Wieck.—A Happy Marriage.—Sad Years.—His Last Hours.................209

CHAPTER XVIII.

Musical Culture.—A Young Girl's Diary.—Stepping-stones.—An Overromantic Student..223

CHAPTER XIX.

The Purpose of the Book.—Technique.—Standard Authorities.—Professional Pianists.—Books on Music.—Conservatories at Home and Abroad.—The Expense of Foreign Study.—Shining Lights.—Authorities used.—How to study Music profitably.................231

INDEX 237

ILLUSTRATIONS.

	PAGE
SONGS OF PRAISE	*Frontispiece.*
ITALIAN SPINET, ORNAMENTED WITH PRECIOUS STONES	14
VIRGINAL	15
PIANO OF ABOUT 1777	17
HANDEL'S HARPSICHORD	19
LUDWIG VON BEETHOVEN	23
YOUNG BACH COPYING MUSIC BY MOONLIGHT	54
JOHN SEBASTIAN BACH	66
GEORGE FREDERICK HANDEL	81
THE BOY LULLI	98
IN THE CHOIR-SCHOOL AT WESTMINSTER ABBEY	101
PAPA HAYDN	107
YOUNG HAYDN SINGING BEFORE THE TWO GREAT MUSICIANS	115
CHRISTOPH RITTER VON GLUCK	126
WOLFGANG AMADEUS MOZART	135
CARL MARIA VON WEBER	179
RICHARD WAGNER	186
FELIX MENDELSSOHN-BARTHOLDY	199
IGNATZ MOSCHELES	208
SCHUBERT SEARCHING FOR THE ARTICLES HIS FELLOW-STUDENTS HAVE HIDDEN	215
MADAME CLARA SCHUMANN	222

THE STORY OF MUSIC AND MUSICIANS.

CHAPTER I.

The Piano-forte.—Its History.—Clavichord, Virginal, and Spinet.—Anecdote of Queen Elizabeth.—An Old Harpsichord.—Piano-forte playing in the Time of Bach, Mozart, and Beethoven.

I WONDER how many young people who sit down to practise or take a lesson at the piano-forte know the story of the instrument now familiar in every household of the civilized world. Look at it as we have it to-day, almost perfect in size and quality and tone. It is capable of producing the fullest and the softest sounds, just as its name indicates, for piano means soft, and forte means loud. Can you realize that little more than a hundred years ago pianos were a rarity? Only one or two makers produced any instruments worthy of the name, and few households possessed one. "But," I can hear my young readers exclaim, "the music *we* play on our pianos—Bach and Hadyn, as well as old English airs—were certainly played on some horizontal instrument." Of course they were, but not on our kind of

ITALIAN SPINET, ORNAMENTED WITH PRECIOUS STONES.

piano-fortes; and the story I am going to tell will take you back far into the sixteenth century, when ladies of rank, and monks and nuns, and some troubadours, had the instruments from which our piano is descended. Such were known as the clavichord and virginal.

The clavichord was perfected about 1500, and the name was derived from *clavi* (a key) and *chorda* (a string); so you see at once that it contained the two principal elements of our piano-forte. Although it went out of use in Bach's day, yet that dear old master, whose gavottes all our young people are playing now, loved to use it. The piano-forte had been invented, but Bach loved his old clavichord. As he sat thrumming it, I think he liked to fancy himself away in the early sixteenth-century days, when Henry the Seventh's court enjoyed madrigals and queer little bits

The Virginal.

of music on the same sort of an instrument. Following the clavichord, we have that graceful, romantic instrument called the virginal. This was an improvement on the clavichord; and towards the close of the sixteenth century we find its name in poetry, romance, biography — indeed in history.

The virginal produced a low, tinkling sort of sound not unlike that of the German zither. Only ladies of quality, musicians, or nuns or monks in convents, performed upon the virginal; and so I think we associate it with all the grace and beauty and the slow stateliness of that romantic epoch.

VIRGINAL.

When I think of a virginal it seems to me to bring many suggestions of rich colors, softly fading lights, the flash of jewels or the movement of white hands, of oak wainscoting and tapestried walls — perhaps some very sad and sorrowing heart, perhaps some young and hopeful one, but always something that is picturesque and dreamy. Perhaps we would not think it so sweet an instrument to-day, but assuredly in the sixteenth century it moved people to very tender, elevated thoughts. Shakespeare wrote of it with deep feeling, and there are some quaint lines of Spenser's about it—

"My love doth sit ... playing alone, careless, on her heavenly virginals."

In 1583 Sir James Melvil was sent by Mary Stuart to England as ambassador, and in his memoirs he relates how he heard Queen Elizabeth play. He says that Lord Hunsden took him up into a "quiet gallery," where, unknown to the queen, he might hear her play. The two gentlemen stood outside a tapestried door-way, from within which came the soft tinkle, tinkle of the virginal. I wish he had told us what the Queen was playing. Presently, it appears, his curiosity to see her Majesty overcame his prudence, and he softly raised the curtain and went into the room. The queen played on "a melody which ravished him," he says, but for some moments did not see any one was listening. Is it not a pretty picture?

At that time the Queen had not lost the charm of youth, and in her splendid dress, with her head down-bent, her figure at the quaint virginal against the rich and sombre colors of the room, must have looked charming to the silent

Scotch gentleman just inside the door-way listening in rapt attention. It is so poetic a picture of the time we can almost hear her music; and if we read on a little farther, we see that the Queen, suddenly seeing Sir James, came forward, remonstrating with him for having come in, for, she

PIANO OF ABOUT 1777.

said, she was not used to play before people, but only to "shun melancholy." Then she sat down upon a low cushion, and honest Sir James, according to the custom of the time, fell upon his knees before her. The Queen, with a truly feminine spirit, inquired whether he thought she or

Mary Queen of Scots played the best. Sir James said that his sovereign played "reasonably for a queen." This answer would not serve to-day, as the Queen of England is one of the most perfect of amateur musicians.

The virginal and spinet belong to the same period. From them, as need of a more elaborate performance grew, we have the harpsichord. A very fine harpsichord looked something like a grand piano, but it had two rows of keys, one upper and one lower. I shall not here go into a description of the harpsichord. It is only needful to say that it was the outgrowth of clavichord and virginal and spinet, and had some of the defects as well as the good points of all three.

Our grandmothers played upon harpsichords. They were tinkling little affairs, yet I fancy that Mozart's and Haydn's music must have sounded very quaint and pleasing upon them. Where have they all vanished to, I wonder? Along with the flowery brocaded gowns, the slender fans, the powder and patches and paint, of that dear old time?

In an old house I once visited, a harpsichord of seventeen hundred and something used to stand neglected and disused in an upper hall. Sometimes we children thrummed waltzes upon it; sometimes I remember our getting out a faded old music-book with the picture of a shepherdess on it, and picking out the funny little songs that were printed there a

hundred years ago. On the fly-leaf of the book was written, in a very flourishy hand, "To Isabel, from J———."
Who was Isabel, and who was J———, we used to wonder.

I can fancy that the music she played to please her

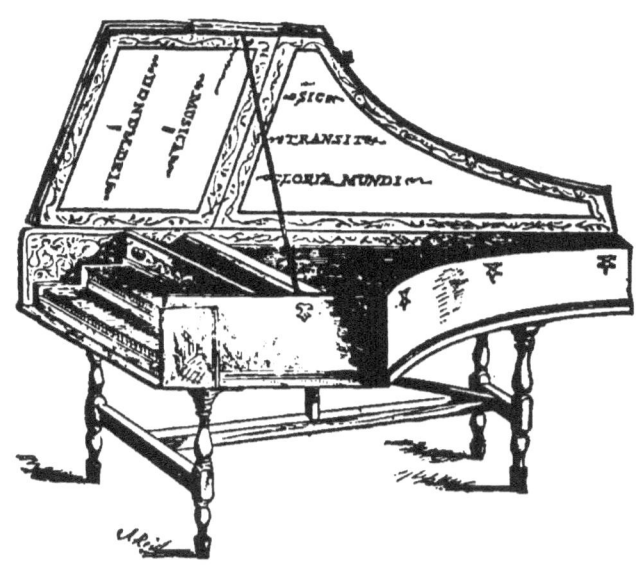

HANDEL'S HARPSICHORD.

mamma and papa, and perhaps her uncles and aunts, was of a very primitive order, for when harpsichords were used young ladies were not at all proficient. Music was then considered a "genteel" sort of accomplishment, and good masters were very rare, and never tried to make their pupils do more than strike the notes correctly and in good "dum-dum" sort of time. Consider our advantages now; and yet I fancy those young people of Isabel's day valued their musical instruction much more than we do ours.

Well, then, from this pretty, picturesque harpsichord period we find ourselves by slow degrees in that of the piano, and I suppose the first thing you will wish to know is how a piano-forte differs from these other instruments of which I have been writing. The principal difference is that the strings are struck with a hammer. About the beginning of the eighteenth century this idea had originated with three men at once — an Italian named Cristofari, a Frenchman named Marius, and a German named Schroter; but all investigators seem convinced that Cristofari was the real originator. His ideas were the best. So, later in the century, when harpsichords began to be thought incomplete, different makers tried to produce something better, and the result was the primitive piano-forte.

At this time the composer Sebastian Bach was in Berlin. Frederick the Great was eager to hear him play; and as that famous sovereign possessed several of the new piano-fortes (or forte-pianos, as they then were called), Bach came one evening to the palace, where a crowd of gay ladies and gentlemen were assembled.

The composer had to go from room to room, trying first

one of the new pianos, then another. These instruments were manufactured in Germany; but, later, English and French pianos took the palm, and about the beginning of this century American ladies were growing proficient in the art of piano-playing—proficient at least for that day. Have you not all seen your grandmammas' music-books, in which "The Battle of Prague" is an honored "piece?" True, there were hundreds of nobler works, but only public performers seem to have attempted them.

Let us see to what degree piano-forte playing had progressed when Mozart died, in 1792, and when the great master, Ludwig von Beethoven, was a young man just entering on his career of work.

To begin with, let us look at the pianos of that day. Although the harpsichord had been greatly improved upon, the keys and strings yet needed something to aid elasticity of touch. In Bach's day it had been the custom to strike the key, drawing the fingers inward slightly, and a suppleness of wrist, which masters think so much of at present, was not considered valuable. But with Haydn and Mozart came a need of something finer in the piano-forte itself, and musicians felt strongly the necessity of an improvement in the instrument whereby they could make more gradual effects. Many efforts to alter the strings and hammers for this purpose proved unsuccessful; but at last the main difficulties were overcome, and before Beethoven's death, in 1827, pianos of various degrees of excellence were in use, with all the desired improvements. To this more than to anything else we owe the improvement in piano-forte playing.

At concerts during this period the piano was largely used, and also in private houses; but lessons from the best masters were rare, and, unless the pupil designed to pursue a musical career, few except the leading people of society studied piano-forte music. In general, the interest in it was not great. Poor Beethoven used often to writhe under what he considered personal slights. A story is told of his once being at the house of Prince —— with Ries, the famous musician. They were invited to play together, and while in the midst of their performance a young nobleman at the lower end of the salon talked quite loudly with his companion. Beethoven glared at him once or twice in vain, and finally lifting Ries's hands from the piano, he called out, "Stop! I will not play for such dogs!" and away he went, in spite of every attempt to an apology.

Such interruptions to music in a drawing-room occur often enough now; but in the beginning of this century, as I said, piano-forte performances were confined to a much smaller number, and naturally appreciation was not general. On the other hand, if a child showed any ability, it was

LUDWIG VON BEETHOVEN.

kept very closely to study. Mozart had pupils who thought nothing of five hours' practice a day; and Beethoven, when a boy, was kept to the piano for hours by means of a good beating every time he left it.

The misery of a musical career at that time was certainly lack of general understanding of the art. Musicians had to procure for themselves noble patrons—rich ladies or gentlemen who would help them on in their divine art, patronize their concerts, get pensions for them, or in some cases offer them homes where they might work unmolested by debt and other domestic trouble. In this way Beethoven lived a great part of the time at the house of Princess Lichnowsky, in Vienna. Mozart was also indebted to some friends for hospitality and influence, and indeed, where the public were so often unappreciative, private patronage had to be sought for, in order that the world might have many of the noble harmonies we possess to-day.

In those days the famous composers or musicians were the only teachers, so that any young student who cared for his work had admirable opportunity to improve. Mozart gave lessons of great length, and seems to have enjoyed them heartily. Haydn had many pupils, one of whom was Beethoven; and we read that he paid Haydn eighteen cents a lesson!

During that period which includes the last years of Mozart's life and the first of Beethoven's, between 1780 and 1792, the way was being laid for Beethoven's grandest work, and yet we can hardly call it a transition state; that is to say, a period of time when any art is undergoing a change which shall effect its whole purpose. But with Beethoven came the perfection of the sonata and the symphony, and all performers, whether in public or private, who attempted his works were compelled to understand technique and the use of their fingers on the key-board; so that we may say, justly enough, that with Beethoven we seem almost to begin a new era in piano-forte music.

I have told you the step upward old Bach made; then Haydn went still farther, preparing the way for Beethoven's perfect work. Mozart's brilliancy and delicacy, both as a performer and a composer, helped the movement on in every way, and during the first quarter of this century a number of men came into fame as masters in execution and composition as well. Indeed, with the beginning of this century piano-playing had reached a period of excellence which allowed a master to indulge all his feelings and ideas in composing for this instrument.

In 1787 Beethoven, then a lad of about seventeen, visited Mozart in Vienna. It was about the time that "Don Giovanni" was being produced, and Mozart's mind was full of its importance, so that the visit seemed of much less consequence to him than to Beethoven. The latter seated himself at the piano, Mozart standing by waiting, good-humoredly, for one of the usual performances of "prodigies" whose parents destine them for the public. But the lad played so brilliantly that Mozart could not but believe that he was executing a well-prepared piece. Beethoven felt this, and eagerly begged Mozart to give him a theme and let him vary upon it.

To this Mozart consented, and presently the room seemed to vibrate with the rush of harmony beneath Beethoven's touch. Mozart listened in silent admiration, and going softly upon tiptoe into the next room, said to some friends assembled there,

"Pay attention to him. He will make a noise in the world some day or other"—a prophecy soon fulfilled.

Beethoven's touch was strong and masterly, but rather heavy, and as his deafness increased, his performances on the piano were almost painful to listen to. His left hand often remained unconsciously on the wrong chord. Mozart never lost the brilliancy of his playing. Haydn, it is said, made the piano "sing;" but to the musicians who followed Beethoven we owe the perfection of piano-forte playing and instruction. Moscheles, Mendelssohn, Chopin, and others realized the highest art in execution. Not very long ago a lady was recounting to me scenes in which, according to her description, Mendelssohn and Moscheles performed actual marvels at the piano, the delicacy and lightness of both their styles reminding her "of a forest full of delicious birds."

In the period of which I speak now—that is, the beginning of this century—you will remember how little public appreciation of art existed, and how hard the greatest men toiled for all they obtained. But love of art is powerful. It will carry any one of you over the roughest places; and, in looking at your well-arranged exercises, try to remember those patient, eager students of eighty years ago, to whom every bit of help came so slowly that we of to-day ought to think our pathway cleared of every thorn.

As time went on, and the interest in the instrument grew, the mechanism of the piano-forte was improved, and at this date (1881) it is considered perfect. Here and there as you play, as you listen to the sounds of the little hammer falling on the strings, let your thoughts wander back to Mary Queen of Scots and Elizabeth of England, with their virginals and spinets—indeed, farther into the realm of poetic, dreamy sound, for beyond these were clavicytheriums, citoles and citherns, dulcimers and psalteries, and in the East, among the people whom we see now in sculpture, a whole line of lyres and harps and lutes.

It may not seem that so far away as early Egyptian days

was the first idea of our piano, yet certainly such is the case. In some far Eastern country you might see, graven in stone of centuries gone by, a figure holding an instrument dimly shadowing that on which you now may play all written music.

CHAPTER II.

Musical Standards Yesterday and To-day.—How to Enjoy the Story of any Art. — A Harmony Class. — A Fascinating Story. — Early Notation.—A Musical Note-book.

"What I want to hear from you," said Von Bulow to a young lady who applied to him for instruction, "is a scale and an arpeggio."

The young lady played the scale of E minor, which is the one used, as a rule, in foreign conservatories as a test for a student's or beginner's capacity. Next the chord of A flat in arpeggio. Again and again she had to repeat them, each time following some especial instruction from the master, and at the end of half an hour she found herself doing them in a manner altogether new to herself, and certainly very much better than she had ever done them before. That half-hour's experience, it seems to me, was invaluable, for it taught her that even when a thing seems to be well done it can always be improved upon, and that a scale which had seemed to her so simple a performance really meant far more than she or most young students appreciate.

Musical Standards Yesterday and To-day. 31

I have heard elderly ladies say that when they were taught music in the first decades of this century, the principal thing was the amount of time they spent practising and the number of pieces which they learned. To perform "The Battle of Prague" or "The Dewdrop" waltz was all that could be expected from amateurs; but in those days only professional musicians really studied. I do not want to say anything against our grandmothers' sincerity, but girls at school or under a governess in those days "took" music as they all took drawing-lessons. Is there any household, I wonder, where souvenirs of the past are cherished, in which there are to be found no pictures of large, flat-looking flowers on pasteboard, or music-books full of painfully unclassical music? Unfortunately, young people to-day "take" music very often with the same inartistic spirit, but happily such rarely perform except for their own families after they leave school. The student whose music nowadays is considered worth anything is the student who thinks and feels and is patient.

Of course every school or conservatory has its own ideas, and I am sure my young readers can tell me of fifty different and perhaps equally excellent methods of teaching used by their different teachers; but the main points, if successful, must be the same, and in this little work my object is not so directly to teach, rather is it to help the student and the teacher by a little outside impetus—something to make study seem more entertaining and worth while.

Directly we begin to think of study as a science and a system the impression is apt to be gained that of necessity the work must be dull and uninteresting; but in point of fact, as I hope to show you, the very science and system of music constitutes its first charm; we will find the history of the science little by little unfolds what makes it most romantic and picturesque, and at last the dullest of five-finger exercises and most tiresome of scales will become invested with a sort of glamour or poetry which will be welcomed by the student who is really zealous as part of what one day will be the real glory of a great achievement.

Now there is nothing gained by going too rapidly in any study. Harmony, thorough-bass, counter-point, all of which mean about the same thing, and which constitute the science of music, are studies which the greatest masters have considered work for a lifetime; but instead of discouraging the young student, this should rather make him see how necessary it is to begin from the very beginning, to understand each day's work at the piano with some of its scientific meaning. All that I hope to do in these pages is to tell you the story of music, as it were, to offer some simple suggestions for piano practice and study, to give the mere rudiments of what is called theory, and to tell you something of the lives of the great composers, the musical influences of their times, and to introduce you to certain of their works.

The world to-day is full of melody; of music such as one hundred years ago could not have been produced. At concerts all over this country, as well as in Europe, the very best music is to be heard; therefore even young people in the audience should bring with them a certain amount of technical knowledge. They should learn enough of theory to understand what is being produced by the great artists of the day. It is all very well to enjoy a fine orchestra, an opera, or an oratorio without troubling one's self about anything scientific connected with it, but really the history of all three is as charming as any fairy tale, and the very science in it, as I hope to show you, has its picturesque side; so that you need never feel it dull work, this following the study of music with a conscientious regard for its higher meanings and its original starting points.

Although study with a view to making music a "career" is different in one sense from study simply for love of it as an art and a personal resource, yet the guiding rules must be the same; and the young student who says to herself, "Oh, but I never should want to play in public!" ought to work with the same spirit as the one who looks forward to a public life, the only difference being in the time bestowed on it. For a professional future six and eight hours a day are required, besides a complete musical life; but two hours a day well employed can work wonders with the amateur student, and with what a feeling of joyful possession does not such a one reach a day when she can really interpret the master's meaning! It ought never to be considered in the light of an accomplishment, only as an art to be acquired for itself, and for the joy there is in acquiring and possessing it. If you do not feel that your music will make you yourself happy, even though you were alone and never to be heard, then do not try to pursue it. Be very certain that no one will care for what you can do in it.

On the other hand, there are many people who for some reason—usually a defective touch or lack of proper feeling for music—can never become executants; yet such a one can nearly always derive the greatest profit and enjoyment from the theoretical study of music. I often wonder why this is not considered a necessary study, independent of musical performance, just as other sciences are taught, for by this means you can open up a whole field of thought and enjoyment.

Listening to music becomes another and newer delight, and besides you can be in possession at least of the science of one of the noblest arts. The best composers have by no means been the best performers—indeed, the very reverse has often been the case, and some of the very best teachers abroad play but indifferently well; that is, the best teachers of technique; for when people speak of taking lessons from Liszt, or Rubenstein, or Bulow, etc., it usually means only playing pieces the notes of which they have learned for these great masters, who correct their style and offer suggestions.

Music as a theory no doubt entails years of study before the whole, or even the suggestion of the whole, is attained, but a great deal that is very satisfactory may be learned in a much shorter time; and to the young student who feels no "instinct" for performance let me suggest fifteen or twenty minutes a day of "theory;" perhaps it may develop the lacking instinct; at all events, if persevered in, it must lead to much satisfaction in hearing and understanding the music on all sides of us to-day.

I well remember the first morning I ever spent in a foreign conservatory of music. I arrived just as the harmony class had assembled. Beside me sat a slim little girl with a very pretty, pale face, and a tired, anxious look. When we had all opened our books, she whispered to me, "May I look over you?"

The expression in her eyes was so piteous that it went to my heart to answer, "You may if you like, dear; only it won't help you. I don't know much of anything myself."

I never shall forget her look as she burst into a silent fit of crying, which for ten minutes stopped the lesson.

Often since I have thought of my little worried companion, who struggled on through the winter, always declaring she could not learn because she could not like it, and I have wondered if there were not a great many young students who feel in the same way.

It is so stupid to hear of semibreves and crotchets and quavers and minims and scales and clefs and scores, and all sorts of terms like "allegro" and "andante" and "con moto" and "adagio," and indeed whole Italian sentences, that used to look to me, when I was a child, like impertinent intrusions into English music.

But have you ever thought whether this system of music which we have to-day may not have had a story—a far-off story almost as entrancing as a fairy tale? I think, had some one told my little friend the story of the system she was toiling to understand, it would all have looked very different, and the study would have been tinged with a real delight.

Now, what I propose to tell you is the history of the notes we use. This is really an introduction to the study of thorough-bass, or harmony; and if you make yourself complete master of the first simple rules or ideas, you will find later that many seemingly difficult things come almost instinctively.

The First Ideas of Harmony.

You know that music to-day is written according to a system, but, as you can readily understand, it was not perfected without a long test of various methods and centuries in which no ideas were sufficiently systematized to create a standard—centuries of crude music and mere experiment, from the days of Saint Gregory, in 590, to the time of John Sebastian Bach, in the middle of the 18th century, when at last even the question of time was perfected. In our own day, however, the study of harmony has become generally appreciated, and masters in the science have quite lately decided upon the best terms to use in expressing certain points which must be impressed upon every student's mind, in such manner as shall make their study not only simpler, but, at the same time, what is called more technical in character. So, for instance, the old-fashioned use of the terms crotchets and quavers is entirely abandoned; whole notes, half notes, quarter notes, etc., take their place, and instead of tones we have steps and half steps, which, as you will see in a later chapter, express better the actual sound of each note in the scale.

The very first ideas of harmony came from the Greeks. In Oriental times there was music at every season of festivity, triumph, mourning, or family rejoicing; but there was no special system for its government, and we suppose that the music of those early days was of a rude character, rendered impressive and effective, however, by the martial spirit or the bravely swelling chorus which inspired and performed it. With the early days of Christianity came a desire for music of a more delicate, although solemn, kind. To express the tenderness of the new law—the law of Christ and his wonderful messages of love—music of a different order seemed needful, and the hearts of men, especially among those early saints, longed for some expression which was poetic and demonstrative of the joyous faith that was within them. Of course their resources were still of the very scantiest. No system of notation had been established, although the letters of the alphabet were used to suggest certain notes; but in the days of St. Gregory we read that musical schools were established in Rome, and we know that he gave his name to a special kind of chant. Church music reached a point in his day whence it could be carried on.

Now we have in old manuscripts some illustrations which show how music was written. The system of using letters of the alphabet, however, came to an end, and was replaced by the use of a series of characters. These are called *neumæ*, and each character had a different name. The first was known as the *virga*, and it was a long single note; the *bivirga* represented two notes, and the *trivirga* three; the *punctus* was a short note, etc.

In old volumes are various illustrations which show how

The Beginning of Written Music.

music was written in that day, and the study of them is curious, since they represent the method which originally preceded the very beginning of our present and perfect system.

Fig. 1 shows the neumæ. There are ten here, but authorities differ as to the number that were really in use. These neumæ were placed over the words, as shown in Fig. 2.

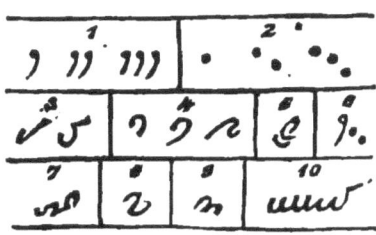

Fig. 1.—The Neumæ.

We are not quite certain what melody they here represent, but the solution given underneath is the probable one.

The first idea of making lines occurred in the year 900. But for a long time only one red line was used, and on this the F note was written; the

Probable Solution of Fig. 2.

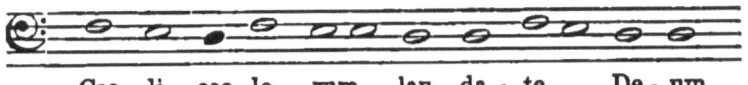

Coe - li coe - lo - rum, lau - da - te... De - um.

grave sounds were placed below this line, the acute ones above it. How this music looked when written you will see in Fig. 3 on the following page.

Early in the tenth century a monk in Flanders, named Hucbaldus, introduced a stave, as we call it, consisting of a great number of lines. At first these lines were not occupied by notes, but by the syllables to be sung, as shown in Fig. 4 on page 41. In order to show whether the voice was to proceed by a tone or a semitone the letters T and S were introduced. One advantage attending this system was that it could be applied to a scale of any extent, and even used for a number of voices singing at the same time.

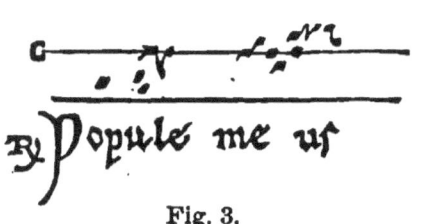

Fig. 3.

PROBABLE SOLUTION OF FIG. 3.

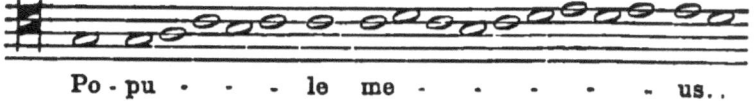

Po - pu - - - le me - - - - - us..

In the Bodleian library at Oxford, England, is a very precious book once used in the Cathedral at Winchester. It is MS., of course, and is believed to have been written during the reign of King Ethelred II., who died in 1016. In it we find music written in two different fashions, as shown in Fig. 5 on page 42.

This, then, was the period of change. We have the sim-

The Score.   41

ple neumæ above the words, and we have actually a four-line stave with notes instead of words.

But up to this time all the notes were the same; no difference in length was indicated, and no one who had not heard the melody could sing it from them. Presently the breve, semibreve, and dot, as shown in Fig. 6 on page 42, began to appear, and thus, little by little, our own system of notation was approached. In 1600, an Italian named Franco de Colonia established a system of

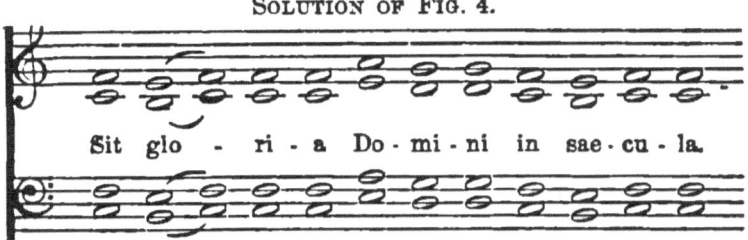

Fig. 4.

SOLUTION OF FIG. 4.

Sit glo - ri - a Do - mi - ni in sae - cu - la.

time, and in or about 1600 the first idea of a score originated.

Do you know what a score is? I was at a concert rehearsal in Paris one day, when a very knowing-looking

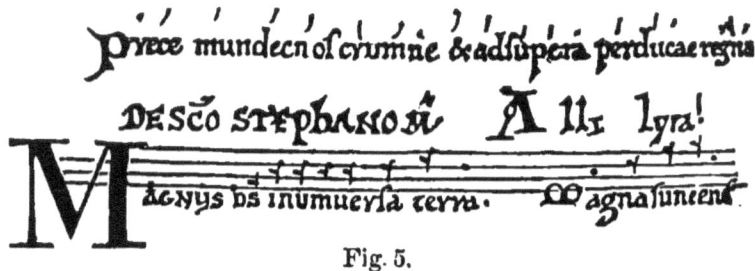

Fig. 5.

young person of about fourteen, with a great deal of fur and velvet on, and a large roll of music, came in with her governess and sat down near me. The orchestra were going

Fig. 6.

to give part of "Faust" with some singing, and this pert young lady turned to her governess, saying,

"Don't you want the score, Miss ——?" and forthwith she handed her the programme.

Now I think it would have been much wiser for this small person to have first been sure what a score was before she talked of it. The origin of the score was in 1600. A composer named Peri published his "Eurydice," and he put the instrumental accompaniment below the vocal part. Then he scored the bars through the stave, connecting the words and music. Hence we call the music and words together the score of the work.

As music began to progress — as oratorios, masses, and operas were written — it became necessary to establish a definite system of time. It was done gradually; but at last, in Bach's day, it was a carefully arranged science — so many beats to the bar, so much value to each note.

A grand science has come from those first queer little attempts at written music which we find it so hard to understand to-day, and yet how grateful we ought to be to the patient people of the seventh and tenth centuries who tried to record some of their musical feelings!

When you sit down to your first harmony lesson, try to remember what a wonderful story those little black notes could tell. It is not dull or colorless work; indeed, if you consider it in the right way, it is like a charming tale in which many characters which make the pages of history vivid and fascinating appear, giving to our work that sense of personality and of tradition — the peculiar interest which comes of any study handed down from one generation to another. All the gradual progression, the slow steps upward, are marked by melody, harmony, chant, or song, so that music as we possess it now may be reckoned as the result of a beautiful and suggestive past. Not a note that you play, not a phrase uttered in your music, not a period rounded and completed but may be made suggestive if you only learn to think of it in this inspiring way.

In this first chapter I want to suggest to you a musical note-book which from day to day may be kept up with profit and much pleasurable interest. Do not attempt to make it too elaborate. From simple beginnings come the best results, and in the study of music, more perhaps than in any other science, everything should be taken slowly and deliberately. No matter how often you go over and over the same things, keep to them until their meanings are fully mastered. Then there will be no confusion in your progress, no necessity for going back.

Begin your note-book with a summary of what you have gathered from this chapter. Put down a list of the early musical terms; add to it such dates as create landmarks in the history of notation. For example, that of St. Gregory, of Hucbaldus, and John Sebastian Bach. Any comments which occur to your own mind it is well to insert; and if you make your book with each alternate leaf of music-lined paper you can gradually add certain fragments of music, so that at the end of a year quite a valuable little book will be in your own possession, and will be an admirable companion to the musical diary of which I will speak later.

CHAPTER III.

How to Feel about Study.—First Steps.—The Key-board.—The Family of Notes.—Staff.—Degrees.—Intervals.—How to Understand the First Rules of Harmony.—Suggestions for Note-book.

WHEN you seat yourself before your piano with a simple piece of music on the stand in front of you, look at the notes on the key-board and those written above on the music, and try to think of them as so many characters, each one with a part of its own to be performed, demonstrating its own individuality by means of your interpretation of it; not to be badly treated or misunderstood by those ten fingers of yours, which with the help of the heart and mind, and, let us hope, some soul too, are to produce all the harmonies of which they are capable.

It is not enough for you to know that the key-board of the piano before you represents merely so many notes whose names, alphabetically arranged, seem so easy to remember. Much more than this must you think of from the very beginning. A grand science belongs to them, and although the study of harmony or thorough-bass cannot be accomplished in all its details without years of study, you can make a point of applying to every musical practice, to every lesson, to every line of music you read and play, a certain amount of technical knowledge which you will find of the utmost assistance when you come to the deeper and closer study of the science itself. Moreover, you will acquire a new sort of interest in your work, by feeling that you bring to each day's progress something which unfolds to you the higher meanings in the art; and it is well in the very outset to impress upon yourself the fact that the first and simplest rules of music are those which must be fixed permanently upon the mind. Try so completely to *understand* what you are learning that there need be no going back over the same ground except by way of refreshing the memory, or making more complete the harmony of your work. Just as in the study of a language it is necessary to learn the alphabet thoroughly, the meaning of each word in a sentence before that sentence can be spoken intelligently, or satisfactorily understood, so in music the very first principles must be mastered before you can hope for any elaborations; and indeed to read and play a simple scale in the best way is to thoroughly understand not only the names of its notes but the reasons for their arrangement and their relationship to each other.

What I wish to tell you about in this chapter is how we

calculate and name that family of black and white notes before you, according to the system of notation used to-day.

To begin with, you know that music is written on five parallel lines. This is called the staff; and on that and on what are called repeated, added, or leger lines are placed the notes which you strike with your fingers. Now, then, the lines and spaces which you see on the staff are called *degrees*, which, as you can see, signifies that from one to another you *progress a degree* each time, for which reason the rule in harmony is that you must count your degrees upward from the very lowest line.

Parker tells us that the distance between two degrees of the scale is called an *interval*, and starting with the note which you know as middle C, and calling that *one*, D is its *second*, E its *third*, F its *fourth*, G its *fifth*, A its *sixth*, and B its *seventh*. Add to this the eighth, and you have the octave, made up of seven distinct sounds, which, according to the latest and best phraseology in music, are known as seven *steps*, the whole forming a *major scale*. This is only the beginning, however, of what you must learn about intervals. There are six kinds of intervals—the perfect, the imperfect, the major and the minor, the augmented and the diminished. These terms have been given after much thought and deliberation, and have each a distinct meaning, which it is well for you to understand and remember

Perfect and Imperfect Intervals.

from the very beginning of your musical practice. For example, let us see what does perfect signify?

Every note when struck produces a certain number of vibrations. Now, then, every note has its octave; for instance, middle C has its octave C in the third space. Strike the first C, and the number of vibrations produced are reckoned as *one*; strike the octave, and the number is doubled; therefore, in reckoning the ratio of sound, the octave is known as number two. This interval is called perfect, as the vibrations are coincident. There are three other perfect intervals, so called because the vibrations produced are so nearly the same that it would be unwise to confuse things by giving them any other name. These are the fourth, the fifth, and the octave, making in our scale four perfect intervals. Now, then, go over this, and striking your first note in any scale, and which is always called the prime, or unison, add to it the fourth or the fifth and the octave, and you have at once your perfect intervals.

To make an imperfect interval, lower the upper note of the perfect interval one half a step. For example, a perfect fifth consists of seven half steps; an imperfect fifth consists of six half steps.

In the same scale the second, the third, the sixth, and the seventh from C, otherwise D, E, A, and B, are known as *major intervals*. Major signifies *greater;* therefore, when applied in this way, it is understood to mean a *greater* interval. For example, the interval from C to D is called a *major* or *greater* second. It consists of two *half* steps, which constitute a *whole* step in sound, or, as we have said, a major second. The interval from C to E is a major third, from C to A a major sixth, and from C to B a major seventh.

Minor signifies *lesser*, and the minor intervals consist of half steps. For example, from C to D flat is a minor or lesser second or interval—it has one half step of sound in it; from C to E flat is a minor or lesser third of three half steps; from C to A flat a minor sixth; from C to B flat a minor seventh. Now, then, you have the major and minor intervals; but in your scale you will remember that the fourth and fifth, and octave, or eighth, are the perfect intervals; that is, they can never be called major or minor.

To thoroughly understand this let me suggest your testing it on the piano. Strike middle C; then strike its second, which is D. Say aloud, "C to D is a major second." Then inquire of yourself what is a major second, how many steps in it, and with the notes before your eyes count them up. You will find that they contain two half steps, each with a sound of its own, and which make a whole step, or major second. What sound lies between C and D natural? The minor second. Strike C again; next to it is D flat, the minor or lesser second. Say to yourself, "How many half steps in that?" Only one. So on through the intervals of which we have been speaking. Then take up the scale as in the illustration below; there you will see written in the musical notation the notes which form the examples which I have given you. Now, then, what is the fixed musical rule for forming a minor interval? It can only be formed from a major interval; that is, the upper note belonging to the major second. Let us say D is lowered half a step, which makes it D flat; take your major third, and in the same way, to make a minor third of it, lower to E flat, and so on.

But, you will ask, are these all the intervals which we have to consider? They are the first and most important ones in beginning musical study, and a very clear knowledge of them is necessary—indeed you cannot too strongly fix them upon your mind; but there are other intervals made from these, and which are known by two names—the augmented and the diminished intervals.

Augmented means increased; therefore, when applied to music, it must mean that the interval is increased. Take your middle C. What is its major second? D. Now, then, how would you make an augmented second of this? All changes of this kind are made out of half steps, a point worth remembering at the start. To augment this major second, then, raise the upper note half a step to D sharp. Therefore an augmented second consists of three half steps of sound—a full step with half a step added. The diminished interval is formed from the minor interval. The lower note instead of the upper is raised half a step. Thus, from C to B flat is, as you know, a *minor seventh*. Therefore, from C sharp (which is the lower note of this raised half a step) to B flat would be a *diminished seventh*, the interval being diminished thus by half a step. If you try this on your piano in the same way as suggested for the major and minor and perfect intervals you will readily see precisely what is meant.

I would advise any young student interested in these suggestions to write out his or her own ideas on the subject, and then to carefully examine with the aid of the piano the illustrations given, and perhaps make out a little table, as it were, of the perfect interval, the major, the minor, the augmented or diminished. In the chapter on notation you had an idea given for a manuscript musical note-book. Supposing you fill one page of this with careful examples of the intervals as you understand them; and in your marginal space it would be well to say that the terms half steps and steps are now used in place of tones, the best judges having decided that they signify the sounds produced more clearly.

CHAPTER IV.

John Sebastian Bach.—His Early Childhood.—The *Gavotte*.—Its Origin. —A Court Dance.—Thé Fugue.—Explanation of this Form of Composition.—Passion Music.—Anecdote of the Basques.—How Mendelssohn revived Bach's Passion Music.

On the 21st of March, 1685, was born to Ambrosius Bach a son, whom he christened John Sebastian, and who, coming of a family famous for their musical ability, was destined to become known throughout the civilized world, not only as a great composer and musician, but as a reformer and developer of the study of technique. His father lived in the quaint town of Eisenach; but before the child had done more than master the rudiments of music and learn to play a little on the violin, his parents died, and his elder brother, Johann Christoph, who was the organist at Ohrdruff, adopted the little boy. He began to study at the Ohrdruff Lyceum, and went ahead in his music with such steadiness that the elder brother, who seems to have been a stern and morose man, forbade the child to do more than his allotted tasks, or to purchase any music for himself, or indeed to indulge any of his impulses in composition.

In the old house at Ohrdruff there was a cupboard which John Sebastian passed many times a day with longing in his heart. Well he knew that on an upper shelf was a rare old book of manuscript music, and it used to seem to him that if he could possess himself of it long enough to copy even a part of its treasures he would feel himself happy as a king. He dared not ask permission lest it be refused, but finally it occurred to him that through the latticed-work panel in the upper part of the door he might squeeze one of his little hands, and pull the book, which was bound in soft parchment, safely through. German children at that time as now were kept so strictly that little John Sebastian rarely escaped some one's watchful eye, but his heart was so strongly filled with this desire that he found an opportunity at last, and climbing up to the latticed part of the panel, contrived to squeeze the precious book through, greatly to his delight. But even then it was hard to know how to copy the music, since candles or light were refused him. So he waited for moonlight nights, and on every one worked hard in his window, finally succeeding in copying the entire book.

I have often thought of the picture of the dear little German boy working away in his old-fashioned room, the moonlight tenderly bathing his head and eager fingers, and illuminating the manuscript page on which he worked.

YOUNG BACH COPYING MUSIC BY MOONLIGHT.

How little he knew, or indeed cared, that nearly two hundred years later all music-loving nations would reverence his name. The work finished, little Bach proceeded to make practical use of it; but judge of his disappointment when his brother, scolding him violently for what he had done, took away the copy he so patiently and lovingly made, and, it is said, burned it before the lad's eyes.

Genius, however, is not daunted by disappointment or even failure. Bach struggled on, learning all that he was taught and much more—in fact drinking in on all sides such music and information as that day afforded; and at the age of fifteen, in the first year of the eighteenth century, we hear of him surprising all the townspeople of Luneburg by his enchanting voice in church.

In return for his leading the boy choir he had his schooling given him, and when holidays came he would walk to Hamburg, a distance of many miles, in order to hear and talk to the famous organist Reinken. This Dutch composer and musician took a great interest in the boy, and gave him freely all the knowledge that he himself possessed, and which Bach absorbed greedily. Meanwhile, in the ducal chapel at Sella, a band of French musicians were engaged, and from them the young student learned chamber and concert music, French in character and performance, and which no doubt strongly influenced him later in the composition of his world-renowned gavottes, passacailles, and sarabandes.

Now, then, let us consider the style of the piano-forte composition and playing at that date. The condition of the instrument was such that music had to be written with a view to its limitations; and as the system of harmony was by no means perfected, the general idea was of a sort of dance music, or the solemn performances of church music not requiring any great breadth of treatment. The organ was the instrument most considered after the violin; but Scarlatti had begun to write music in a newer or more original style, and no doubt his work was very suggestive to Bach. The actual piano-forte was invented in his day, but Bach always clung to the clavichord, on which he said he could express himself as he desired; and his manner of playing was remarkable for its entire correctness, and at the same time brilliancy, so that we may infer that many performers of that day drew their inspiration from him, since, both in composition and execution, he was undoubtedly original. Determined to compose piano-forte music of a higher order than anything which had been written, he set himself to the development of a firmer basis of theory, and what is known as counterpoint, and to him we owe much of our present knowledge of time in music. He also composed with direct reference to and following of all the rules of harmony then known, and those which he himself worked out and developed, so that at the present day no studies are better for the beginner, or even advanced student, than those of John Sebastian Bach. With the gavotte, and other pieces of similar character, Bach's name is indelibly associated. He made them not only fascinating, but wrote them in so scientific and masterly a manner that they offer endless instruction and suggestion to musicians to-day. Some of the gavottes were in single pieces, some in what are called suites, or sets of short pieces of music; and the other day an old friend of mine showed me a fragment of a manuscript music-book which was part of a gavotte written for some festive occasion, I believe, in his native town. In a French gallery there is a picture of splendidly-dressed ladies and gentlemen dancing the gavotte. They wear the costume of the latter part of the seventeenth century; they have smiling faces; they flourish large fans, and wear high-heeled slippers which they lift gracefully—for the gavotte was a very brilliant dance in its movement.

The name came from a people in Dauphine known as Gavots. They danced it more wildly than the stately people of Louis's court, but the music of every gavotte seems to me to be best suited to them. One can fancy them on their village green clattering away to the quaint, gay music, flinging their arms about, or beating time with their hands.

But when the gavotte was introduced into the upper classes, and with it various other dances of the people, it became more refined, dignified, even more serious.

It is always well, even for beginners, to understand the principle on which any kind of music is written. You will find your practising much more interesting if you look deeper than the mere sounds. Suppose we take some simple gavotte and examine into the way it is written. Here, for instance, is the first strain in one of Bach's most popular gavottes:

THE GAVOTTE.

Now let us see what the few rules created for its composition are. They are these:

It must be in common time, which really means equal time—two or four beats to the bar—although the term is generally applied to that of four quarter notes to the bar, marked by the Italian C.

The movement is rather quick, and it is generally in two parts. These parts are, in accordance with a custom peculiar to old dances, repeated.

Originally the gavotte consisted of four bars in the first part and eight bars in the second; but if the gavotte is only one of various parts of a suite, no fixed number of bars is given. Now, as a general rule, the gavotte begins on the third beat of the bar, so that you will see, if you calculate, that each part must finish with a half-bar containing a quarter note.

I know that to many of my young readers this may sound very dull and useless, but if you will only give a little careful study to a few rules which apply to your first "pieces," lessons in real harmony and thorough-bass will seem much more interesting to you later on. The chaconne and the passacaille, the passaglia and the sarabande, are all dances of about the same period as the gavotte, and have certain governing principles. The chaconne is slow, and is usually written in the major key.

The passacaille is written in the minor key. What is called the theme in the chaconne is invariably in the bass; in a passacaille it may be in any part. The passacaille has a very curious kind of interest, since in the last century composers made use of it to show their skill—what is known as contrapuntal skill. It must consist of a short theme of two, four, or eight bars. Bach, Frescobaldi, and Handel all wrote famous passacailles.

The sarabande is more stately in its movement. It was

a popular dance in the sixteenth century, and some say it was introduced then by a famous dancer called Varatanda. I think that it might often have formed part of very picturesque scenes in the sixteenth and seventeenth centuries, when people were full of a certain kind of poetry, and enjoyed whatever was splendid and stately. Sometimes dancers were hired to perform it; sometimes ladies and gentlemen of quality danced it for their sovereign.

Old songs are full of references to sarabandes as being danced at times when sadness, or even deep regret, filled the minds of the performers; so that we may picture it as a slow, pathetic movement, with melancholy and sweetness in its train.

In 1723 Bach was appointed cantor of the Thomas-Schule, in Leipsic, and organist and director of music in the principal churches. There he remained until his death, in 1750, and the organ played by him in the old Thomas-Kirche is still in use there, and seems to breathe forth suggestions of the dear master who, even when afflicted by blindness, loved to spend hours before it, improvising or producing all sorts of the harmonic changes in which he delighted, and entrancing his hearers by some of his grand *fugues*.

A fugue is a piece of music in which one part after another seems to *chase* the subject or *motive;* it is derived from the Latin *fugare*, to put to flight, and it is written according to a fixed plan, and involves all sorts of harmonic forms, which you will the better appreciate with a further study of thorough-bass. What are known as canon, imitation, and double counterpoint are included in it. There is first a subject started; then what is called the *answer;* then the counter-subject; then the stretto, which is an imitation of the subject, but in *closer time*, and is supposed to give a sort of *sweep* to the climax. After this may be added what is called a codetta, which is a little "tail-piece," as it were, and gives a greater idea of finish or completeness—an *episode* and a *code*, which is a larger kind of codetta.

There are fixed rules to be observed in the composition of the fugue, but their details would not come within the limits of our present purpose; some you may remember when you begin the real study of harmony, and may as well be given now.

When the *subject* has the *tonic*, the answer should have the *dominant;* when the subject has the third of the tonic, then the answer must have the *third* of the dominant, and *vice versa,* and so on. When the fugue is in the minor, and the subject has the *interval of the diminished seventh*, that interval must come in unchanged in the answer. In either major or minor, if the subject goes from the dominant to the sub-dominant in the upper octave, the *answer* must constitute the interval of an octave. Now, would it not be a profitable employment to make a little of this out on your piano, and make notes of the same in your manuscript-book with a line or two from some characteristic gavotte and fugue—just enough to clearly indicate in musical writing the *main rules* to be employed.

Still another form of famous music is specially associated with the name of John Sebastian Bach. This is what we know as the *Passion music*.

I was staying once in a little sea-bound village just on the borders of Spain, and there I became very much interested in talking with two of the country people: one was a pretty young peasant woman of the Basque race; the other a lad, also a Basque, who spent most of his time fishing. From them I heard a great deal about the curious allegorical and religious performances which from time to time they had taken part in. These were plays given in the public squares at certain seasons. The characters were usually chosen from the Bible, and the plot of the play, or rather its chief idea, would be some biblical scene.

From time immemorial these plays had been given, and the ideas of the people were too simple to make them wish the custom altered. No form of dramatic or musical representation is older, and so we ought to have great respect for them, knowing they have come down from very pious, early times.

In some ways the Passion music, which I hope we will now hear every year in America, has its origin in the same feeling which influenced the writers of those early Christian plays; and although its form varies now very much, it still keeps the original idea — that of describing in music the story of the Passion of our Lord.

We use music for so many lighter purposes that sometimes people shrink from the idea of associating it with anything so sacred. Yet, after all, what art is more fitting to speak to us of what ought to be dearest to our hearts? The grand and simple story of His life is not any less beautiful because we listen to it sung by pure voices with the accompaniment of harmonious sounds.

Passion music seems to have had its origin in the fourth century, when S. Gregory Nazianzen first prepared it in real form. None of this music is preserved, but we know that it was very widely sung in the early Church.

A great many different ideas followed these first ones down to the time of the Reformation. Finally the idea of a more perfect form of Passion music worked its way on to about 1728, when Sebastian Bach conceived the idea of writing a complete Passion oratorio. His plan was to give the exact words of the Gospel as far as possible, with good choruses, some recitatives, and four-part chorales.

The great musician succeeded almost beyond his own

expectations. It is impossible to describe the tremendous and sublime effect of this great work. It is written for two orchestras and two choirs; it seems to contain every variety of musical expression, and the whole thing breathes such a purely devotional spirit that it is like the prayer of some strong Christian heart.

Bach was at the time organist of the old church of St. Thomas, in Leipsic, as well as cantor of the school, and so he had every opportunity of bringing out his work in perfection. It was produced for the first time on Good-Friday, 1729. Between the two parts a sermon was preached, and it is recorded that the entire service produced a wonderful effect upon all present.

But later the interest in his marvellous music seemed to flag. For a century it lay untouched; and as it will undoubtedly continue to be given in America, I think the story of how it was unearthed will prove interesting to the young musicians whom I am addressing.

During the winter of 1827 Felix Mendelssohn, then about eighteen years of age, was living in Berlin, in his father's household. It was a charming one, the brothers and sisters being united by affection and many sympathies. They seem to have been equally fond of music, painting, and literature. Naturally such a delightful young circle drew into it many agreeable friends. Felix's chosen companion was

Edward Devrient, an artist whose voice was exquisite, and whose knowledge of music was quite equal to that of Felix's. Every Saturday Devrient and other friends used to meet at Felix's home to practise vocal music; and as Felix had a great enthusiasm for "old Bach," he one day suggested their trying the Passion music, which was unknown, except in name, even to these ardent students. So they began upon it, and their enthusiasm grew as they learned, page after page, the various parts, as Devrient says, filling them with new reverence for the Bible story.

It occurred to Devrient to produce the music in public. The little circle was startled by such a venturesome idea. Mendelssohn declared it would be a failure. Old Zelter, his teacher, was the most influential musician in Berlin, and Felix well knew how much opposition he would have to expect from him.

But Devrient persisted. He knew that if Felix once undertook it all would go well. At last the two friends decided to go to Zelter and see what he would say to their plan. Devrient has left a very entertaining description of this interview.

Zelter lived in the Musical Academy; they found him at home, but sitting with his long pipe in a cloud of smoke. Out of this he looked at the two young men, exclaiming,

"Why, how is this? What do two such fine young fellows want with me at this early hour?"

"Now," writes Devrient, "I began my well-studied speech about our admiration of Bach, whom we had first learned to prize under his guidance.... He enlarged upon the difficulties of the work, which required resources such as existed in the Thomas-Schule when Bach himself was cantor there— the necessity for a double orchestra and double chorus.... He became excited, rose, put aside his pipe, and began walking about the room. We, too, rose. Felix pulled me by the sleeve; he thought nothing more could be done."

But Devrient persisted, and finally Zelter agreed "to speak a good word for them." When they left the room Felix laughingly called his friend an arch-rascal. "Anything you like, for the honor of Sebastian Bach," exclaimed Devrient, as they went into the street.

They began the rehearsals, the arrangement of the score, all the fascinating, though severe, labors which belong to the preparation of any such work. When they went to engage the solo singers, "Felix," says Devrient, "was child enough to insist on our being dressed exactly alike."

They wore "blue coats, white waistcoats, black neckties, black trousers, and yellow gloves," the fashionable attire of the time; but an idea may be had of how economically a young German lad of that period was brought up by Devri-

JOHN SEBASTIAN BACH.

ent's story that, Felix's pocket-money having run out, he loaned him a thaler (about one dollar) to buy his gloves, upon which Madame Mendelssohn was quite displeased, saying, "Young people should not be assisted to extravagance."

It was just one hundred years since Bach's music had last been heard, and this idea filled the two young men with enthusiasm. They could think and talk of nothing else. One day, as they crossed the Opern Platz, Felix stood still, suddenly exclaiming, "To think that it should be an actor [Devrient] and a Jew that give back to the people the greatest of Christian works!"

The performance was in every way successful. Zelter's prejudices vanished, and all Berlin went wild over this revival of an interest in Bach. A second concert was called for, and in other towns the music began to be studied and produced. What seems to me best worth recording of this is the fact that by perseverance in the right direction these two young men did a lasting favor to all the world.

Devrient sang the part of Christ. He says of it: "Deeply affected by the work as it proceeded, I sang with my whole soul and voice, and believed that the thrills of devotion that ran through my veins were also felt by the rapt hearers."

Truly, as Devrient says, we owe thanks to that year 1829,

in which the "light of Bach's greatest music" was given to us.

At Felix Mendelssohn's funeral, in 1847, Devrient must have had sad and sweet memories of this time of their youth. Among the various selections of sacred music sung on that occasion the final chorus of the Passion music, "We sat down in tears," was given with most solemn effect.

CHAPTER V.

Rhythm and Time.—Bach's Developments.—A Simple Explanation.—Keys and their Families.—A Bach Fugue.—Minor Scales.—Modulations.—Accidentals.—A few Words about Signatures.—Why Handel and his Contemporaries discarded the lowest Note of the Signature.

THE growth of counterpoint was not a very rapid one, and various composers strove to perfect it, working out by means of their own genius and technical ability certain matters connected with it which, in the beginning, were very often too confused to be of much service to the student. John Sebastian Bach devoted his attention earnestly, as you have seen, to certain points in harmony. To the question of *time* he gave much attention; and as with this came a necessity for rhythm, and as he united to his studies in this direction that of a careful regard for the keys in which his works were written, his compositions afford the young student admirable opportunity for thoughtful and interesting work.

In ancient music time or rhythm was determined without any bars being marked or drawn across the stave. The value of the notes determined the rhythm, but, as can readily be imagined, this gave rise to much confusion, and in the sixteenth century Henry Lawes was the first English musician who regularly made use of bars in his composition. It was only after this period that rhythm in music began to be regularly understood, and it is well for us, in the very beginning of musical practice or study, to thoroughly understand the meaning of all such terms—a just comprehension of them being most useful to any pianist; my own belief being that the very knowledge of the origin and meaning even of a bar line, or of the length of a single note, may influence the student's performance; for directly the spirit of harmony and of melody together is infused into the work, new lights seem to come upon it, and we can no longer be simply imitators or perform mechanically with a view to making a fine effect only, for the higher and at the same time more technical meanings of the page before us are understood. Rhythm has been defined in various ways, but it may be said to be the metre of music. The intervals of steps and half steps have been given a specified value in order to produce the sounds with regard to harmony and melody, and to create what is known as time. Time in music is an expression of rhythm, and rhythm is the "systematic grouping of notes with regard to duration." To rhythm time and accent stand in the same relation, so an admirable authority tells us, that *metre* bears to quantity in poetry. When we speak of the fine rhythm of any composition, we mean that the composer has arranged his musical ideas in a graceful manner. The spirit of the work depends largely upon the swing or rhythm which the composer suggests, and which it is the part of the player to appreciate and express. This being addressed to young pianists, I dwell more upon the sentiment in the meaning of the word than its more purely technical definition. To give this swinging rhythmical utterance in your music, and at the same time to preserve directly the time in which the work is written, should be a never-failing effort on the part of all real students, however moderate their ambition or performance. When you use a term, however, in its strictly critical sense, be careful to thoroughly understand its meaning. There is no trace of rhythm in barbarous music. The different masses of notes, so to speak, which are arranged or divided by time into groups of equal duration, did not exist in any fashion sufficiently orderly in ancient days to have a rhythmical meaning. No one verse, so to speak, in music was begun and ended completely enough, or with sufficient system, to make this possible. Accent and time were necessary before rhythm could be in use. When the upper figure which marks the time in which a piece is to be played is an even number it is in direct rhythm, and the leading accent always comes on the first beat of each measure. The secondary accent occurs when the movement in which a piece is played is *moderately* quick, and falls on the middle of the bar. When the movement is very slow, you may often subdivide these accents. If it be very quick, a primary accent may only fall upon every other bar; but much of this must be determined by the musical taste and feeling of the player. When, however, a piece begins with a fraction of a bar, the utmost care must be taken in regard to the accents employed. Every dot or rest is of consequence in reading or playing, and belongs to the study of rhythm; to read or play "following the marks" strictly is considered an evidence of what may be called good breeding in music, and should be taken into consideration by every student from the first note of the first piece learned. The gavotte, as I have told you, begins almost always on the third beat of the bar, ending with a half bar containing a quarter note. Study even a few lines of one of Bach's gavottes with distinct reference to time and rhythm, taking it as you would so much poetry, and you will have the best example needed for our subject. And for the study of key-notes, with the tonic, the dominant, and, at the same time, the interval of the diminished seventh, nothing could be better than one of Bach's simplest fugues.

When we speak of the *key* in which any piece of music is written, we mean a "family of tones," as it were, which are all in a fixed state of relationship to *one leading tone*, which is called the *key-note*, or, better still, the *key-tone*. For example, if a piece of music is said to be in the " key of C," it means that C is the key-tone from which the piece is built up; and as each key has its own progressions—family laws and rights and meanings—so each must have its family name. In writing music, of course all sorts of rules must be observed in regard to these different families. By following them strictly harmony is preserved, the sounds are perfect, the strains pleasing in proportion to the care paid all these many laws of music; and while the young student cannot expect to appreciate fully all these, there should be an earnest desire to understand *leading principles*.

A scale of any kind presents the material of a *key*, and the *leading note* or tone is the *key-note* or *key-tone*, called the *tonic*. All keys are either *major* or *minor*, and two have been chosen as the *models* on which all others are formed—C in the major, A in the minor. The *pitch* may be different in different keys, but, as you will see, the structure or manner of building your tone ladder up is exactly the same in all major keys and in all minor keys.

Now, then, the *tonic* is of the greatest importance, as, without knowing that, we would not have any idea in what key any piece of music was written; and in order to preserve the unity of sound, the finish of any melody is always *on the tonic* note, or else on the major or minor, third or the fifth, and in the close of the piece, if in a chord, the lowest note *must* be the tonic.

The next tone of importance to your key is the *dominant*. Using C as our model, take the fifth from that, *i. e.*, *G*, and you have the *dominant*. The chord of the *dominant* is the *controlling chord*, because, in making the modulation from one key to another, the moment you reach the dominant you are the same as *in* the key, and it is the chord which exercises most influence over the progression. The *sub-dominant* is the *fourth* from the key-note going up; reverse it, or turn it down, and it is the fifth. (Exercise this upon your piano, and it will become clear to you at once.)

Now, then, each family of tones of course has its relations. When we speak of a *related key*, we mean one in which there is but one note of difference. For example, take your key of C. *G* is its *related key*, because there is in the scale of G but *one* note of difference, F sharp.

F natural is a related key of C, because there is only the difference of B flat, and these keys work in harmony together, although of course, by making your *progressions* properly, you pass from them into every other.

Now, for a little bit of study go back to your fugue of old Bach. If the *subject* has the *tonic*, or begins with it,

Formation of the Scale.

what is the answer? Study this out easily and carefully, as a means of impressing the significance of the terms upon your mind.

The minor scale is formed in the following fashion: Every major scale, to begin with, has its relative minor, and that minor of course must have its tonic or key-note. To determine this you must count down from the key-note of the major scale three half steps, otherwise to a *minor third.* For example, take the key of G. Three half steps below you have your minor third, which is E; therefore E is the tonic or key-note of the relative minor of G, and it starts the scale known as E minor. If a piece is written in the minor, however, the *signature* is precisely the same as in the major. For instance, in this case, the key being G major, there would be one sharp, F, in the signature. To determine, however, that the piece is in the minor, see whether the major *seventh* from the key-note of E *is not always raised*, otherwise *D sharp*, as this is invariably the case in all minor scales.

Take now the key of C; count down three half steps, you have *A;* A, therefore, is the prime unison or tonic of your minor scale. Now let us see how the scale is formed, remembering that *all minor scales are built up on the same principle.* B, which is a *major second,* follows; next C, which is a *minor third;* D, a *perfect fourth;* E, a *perfect fifth;* F, a *minor sixth;* G sharp, an accidental, and your major seventh; and A of course the octave. Now you will observe that the seventh, by what is called a chromatic alteration, is always made major, raising it a half step. In playing a minor scale *up* from the lower note to the upper, no one plays the *minor sixth,* for the simple reason that it is hard for voices and impossible for some instruments to take it, and for this reason it is made *major;* otherwise F sharp in the key we are considering, because that *augmented second* from F natural to G sharp is very difficult for voices to reach accurately, and it would be impossible, as I say, for certain instruments. Returning, however, in *the descent* of the scale, this does not apply, so you may play your scale correctly, according to the given rule of harmony; for instance, using your G sharp and F natural.

Now, if this sounds very puzzling it will be a proof that in your study of the *intervals* you have not sufficiently impressed upon your mind exactly the meaning of the term used, or learned how to calculate your degrees, and it will be an excellent evidence to you of the necessity of taking things slowly and carefully, and thoroughly understanding each division of your labor as far as you go.

The minor is employed with admirable effect by all composers, deepening the melancholy, sentiment, pathos, or intensity of their work, and in some themes being indispensable.

Illustrations of Signature.

Take your twelve scales, and you will find that they are all built up on precisely the same rules.

When a piece is written partly in one key and partly in another, it is said to be *modulated*, but in any and every case it *must* return to the original key, and all the notes which do not by rights belong to the key — the flats and sharps which would occur in the key that it goes into for a while — are written and are called *accidentals*. Occasionally the key into which the piece changes is sufficiently remote from the original to make it worth while to entirely alter the signature; for example, supposing the key be E-flat major, your signature would be thus:

Modulating or changing to E major, the signature would be altered thus:

The original flats would be cancelled or turned into *naturals*. When the modulations are only into a very nearly related key — for instance, into the key of the dominant, which is, you know, the fifth from the tonic — then no alteration is needed, for the accidentals would be so few. For this reason we find the second movement of a sonata in the dominant requires no change in the signature.

The following shows you a table of the sharp and flat signatures now in use:

Some composers in the last century dropped the last sharp or flat in the signature, and marked it throughout the piece as an accidental. The reason given by good critics for this is that they desired thereby to call the attention of the player more particularly to it, as it is regarded as the *most necessary note in the signature*, and without that you could not distinguish the key from the one just preceding it. For example, in the key of D flat the last flat, G, is the only one which distinguishes it from its predecessor, A flat, and it is accordingly of greatest importance. Part of the "Messiah" is written out in the way I have mentioned, leaving out this essential note in the signature. An excellent suggestion for your musical note-book would be the mention of certain pieces where the signatures vary. Give the original key, mention the modulations, the accidentals, etc., and especially note the use of major or minor.

CHAPTER VI.

George Frederick Handel. — An English Country-house. — A Young Lady's Impressions of the great Composer in 1711.—"Tweedledum and Tweedledee."—"Rinaldo" and other Operas.—A Friendly Coterie.—"The Harmonious Blacksmith."—"Mr. Handel" in Dublin.—Mr. Dubourg.—The First Performance of the "Messiah."—Last Days.—Definition and History of the Oratorio.

ONE May morning, in the year 1711, the drawing-room of an English house not far from Windsor Castle presented an animated appearance. A distinguished visitor was expected, and the three young ladies of the family, attired in their best flowered chintzes, and with their most approved of company manners, were gathered in the large bow-window, quite breathless with anxiety as to how this morning call would be on all sides enjoyed. One of the daughters of the house had been in Germany attached to the Hanoverian court, where she had made the acquaintance of the guest now expected, George Frederick Handel, the musician and composer, who is perhaps best known to-day for his famous oratorio of the "Messiah."

When George I. became King of England he continued his interest in Handel, and was the means of inducing the musician to visit his adopted country, and the eldest Lady G——, having met her former teacher drinking tea at Windsor, an invitation for a morning at her father's country-house quickly followed; and we may fancy a flutter among these simple maidens, whose musical ability was of the most limited order, and who, from what they had heard, were inclined to feel rather afraid of the burly, hot-tempered genius just then absorbed in writing Italian opera music, which was all that the fashionable world of London in that day cared for. Young Lady G—— had passed a morning with the daughters of the Prince of Wales, whom Mr. Handel was teaching to write music, and I have no doubt that the young people enjoyed a little gossip over the two factions into which society was then divided. Operas were quite a novelty. Fine ladies and gentlemen crowded the green-rooms of the opera-house, chatted and talked at the wings as if they were in a drawing-room. Fashion governs nearly everything, and Handel, whose soul was full of grand ideas, had to content himself at first with working upon an opera in order to please the public. He wrote "Rinaldo" in fourteen days, and it was produced at Drury Lane with a splendor that created great excitement throughout London. We never hear the opera of "Rinaldo" now, but one of its airs is very beautiful. "Lascia ch' io Pianga" lingers in the heart of every one who hears it.

GEORGE FREDERICK HANDEL.

As soon as he became famous, and very much the fashion, Handel roused the jealousy of petty people, and opinions differed to such an extent that society actually took sides— one favoring a distinguished musician named Buononcini, and the other Handel. The war raged, and during it a wit and poet named John Byron wrote the following verse, which has since been famous:

> "Some say, as compared to Buononcini,
> That Mynheer Handel's but a ninny;
> Others aver that he to Handel
> Is scarcely fit to hold a candle.
> Strange all this difference should be
> 'Twixt tweedledum and tweedledee."

The Ladies G—— belonged no doubt to the "tweedledum" faction, and so we may fancy Mr. Handel received in this quaint drawing-room where I took a cup of tea not long ago, and heard the story—with all the pretty airs and formality of the period. Presently he is led away to the music-room, where was a fairly good organ, upon which he performed, greatly to the delight of his hostess and her family, and no doubt with much more enjoyment for himself than if he had been obliged to exchange compliment and pretty nothings in the drawing-room below. That the visit was considered an honor, indicating the feelings towards the musician, is shown by the entry in young Lady G——'s diary, and which, in faded characters, seems to bring up a pleasant scene of the past:

"This morning came Dr. Handel, the great musician. He played on the organ for us, and we were in a state of great joy all the time. L—— could hardly keep from crying, but I know not whether it was most with the musicke or the honor. He says the Prince of Wales's daughters have a very pretty talent for musicke, and one of them pleases him much."

Far back of this time, however, Handel could remember a childhood in which his music had to find utterance under protest. He was born on February 23, 1685, in Halle, Saxony. His father was a good surgeon, but he abhorred music. As soon as little George Frederick began to show an aptitude for it his father took him away from school, lest any one of his companions should teach him his notes. Whether among the teachers or scholars I do not know, but the boy found a friend who gave him a little dumb spinet, and this he secreted in an attic, contriving not only to learn his notes from it, but to use his fingers in practising. Still his father opposed him; but at last his genius was made evident owing to an accidental visit.

The elder Handel was invited to visit his son, who was in the service of the great Duke of Saxe-Weissenfels, and young George, knowing that music was always to be heard, if not learned, in that place, determined to accompany his parent. Dr. Handel set out in his carriage, but after the first mile looked around to discover his little son running, as hard as his small legs would carry him, after the carriage. At this the father's heart relented; the child was picked up, and, promising to behave well, taken to the castle, where the duke was willing enough to allow him to remain for a day or two.

In the old castle many of the inmates were musical, and the boy, left much to his own devices, soon made friends with them, and obtained easy access to the music-rooms and the chapel organ. One afternoon, the services being ended, little Handel sprang on to the stool before the organ and commenced playing, unconscious that the duke was lingering below. His astonishment and delight were great when he was summoned to the duke's presence, and his father sent for to explain why musical advantages had not been given him. After this there could be no question as to the boy's future.

Old Dr. Handel gave his consent to his son's musical education, and almost from that moment George Frederick Handel became known as a musician.

I cannot tell you anything more of his childhood or his youth but that he studied hard, and, like all geniuses, was humble while he was learning.

We must skip over many years to the time when he went to England, for there he produced his greatest work, and to this day the English reverence him as their own. He had visited Italy, and in Venice met the best musicians of the day. Of this winter an amusing anecdote is related. The carnival season was at its height, and Handel being masked at a certain ball, seated himself uninvited at the harpsichord and began playing, improvising so that his identity would not be known. The crowd of masks were not attracted especially until suddenly a brilliant figure appeared in one of the door-ways and stood transfixed by the music. This was Scarlatti, son of the first great musician of that name, and himself the leading harpsichordist in Italy. After a few moments' silence he strode across the room, calling out, "*This is either the devil or the Saxon!*" Handel being known throughout Venice as "The dear Saxon" (*Il caro Sassone*). Handel removed his mask, Scarlatti doing the same, and from that moment the two were firm friends.

A few years later we find him in England, where, having written his opera of "Rinaldo," he was obliged to arrange it all for the harpsichord, and throughout the length and breadth of the country it was played. Perhaps no musical composer's work — unless it be that of the writers of the English opera to-day—ever was so generally played, sung, whistled, danced to, marched by, or buried with as was Handel's during the period of his English popularity.

Handel made friends, or perhaps I should say associates, wherever he found appreciation of music, and so, in a long room over a table in Clerkenwell Green, he had many a delightful morning of music with congenial friends, none the less appreciated because they were entertained by one Thomas Britton, the owner of the stables, a coal-heaver who had a passion for music, and delighted in welcoming Handel, for whom he procured a chamber-organ and various stringed instruments, he himself performing very well on a viol de gamba. A painter of the day sketched the coal-heaver and his guests, and made a picture of one evening's scene there when Handel was playing "The Harmonious Blacksmith" for such a company as Pope the poet, the Duchess of Queensbury, Dr. Pepusch, Colley Cibber, Buononcini, and many others of that period of genius and splendor.

When Handel began to work on his oratorios he had to contend against a strong feeling. "Saul," in which occurs the famous Dead March, was produced in 1739. (This march is noticeable to the student as being one of the few very stately and solemn pieces of the kind which is written in a major key.) "Israel in Egypt" followed this, but Handel's success in England seemed to have considerably abated.

The Irish papers announced in November, 1741, that "Dr. Handel arrived in the packet-boat from Holyhead, a gentleman universally known by his excellent composition in all kinds of music.

In Dublin he took people by storm, and be it said to the credit of the Irish taste in music, which is too slightly appreciated even to-day, that his best work was what attracted most attention in the city of Dublin. There, on the 13th day of April, 1742, Fishamber Street was crowded to excess, the doors of the new music-hall thronged, noblemen and ladies of "quality" competing eagerly with people of the middle and even lower classes for places in the concert-room. On that day, as was announced, "Mr. Handel's new oratorio, 'The Messiah,' was to be performed for the first time." It is interesting to us to know that the chief singers on this first occasion were Mrs. Cibber, Mrs. Avolio, and Mr. Dubourg. Of the latter an amusing story was told me by a well-known musical director, who showed me Handel's *pitch-pipe*. Dubourg was fond of introducing cadenzas into his music, whether sung or played. In vain Handel, as director, tried to keep the artist strictly to his text. At a special concert, when Dubourg in his most elaborate manner began indulging some fantasies of the kind, Handel stood up and called out,

"Welcome home, Mr. Dubourg! welcome home again,

sir!" which recalled the discomfited Dubourg to his proper place.

So successful was the oratorio that the whole of Dublin rang with his praises. The anxiety to obtain places became so great that the ladies of rank in the capital agreed for the time being to go without hoops so that an additional number of people could be admitted in the audience, and England, which had for some time neglected and imbittered the composer, woke to the fact that a very great man indeed had been in their midst. Still on his return to London a great many in the fashionable world tried to interfere with his success. The oratorio of "Samson" was produced, but failed, and it was not until 1746-7 when "Judas Maccabæus" appeared, that the tide seemed to turn in his favor, and to this day shares some of the perennial honor offered to the "Messiah." "Joshua," "Solomon," "Susanna," and "Theodora," followed this, and Handel was again on the pinnacle of success.

He lived very quietly, with but few and simple amusements, smoking his pipe and drinking his beer moderately with a few intimate friends, and caring but little for the opinions floating about him. In 1751 he was at work upon a new oratorio, "Jephthah," and was attacked with that blindness from which it seems so many famous musicians have been doomed to suffer. In 1752 his eyesight failed entirely, but it is said that his nature became much softer, gentler, and more kindly in every way after this terrible affliction was pronounced incurable. To all sorts of charitable institutions he contributed liberally, and played frequently on the organ at the Foundling Hospital for some charitable purpose. He had no desire to have his life prolonged; on the contrary, it is said that during that last year he frequently expressed a hope that he might die upon Good-Friday; "in hopes" he said, "of meeting his good God, his sweet Lord and Saviour on the day of his resurrection."

On the 6th of April, 1759, he conducted an oratorio of the "Messiah" at Covent Garden. Late on Good-Friday night in the same year he quietly passed away, and so in his last earthly hour fulfilling his dearest wish, and leaving behind a record of unfailing Christian goodness, an untiring devotion to work, and music which will live as long as the voices and hearts and hearing of any people exist.

The oratorio, strictly speaking, is a sacred poem sung by soloists and a chorus, and with a full orchestra accompaniment, but without any stage or scenic effect, such as scenery, costume, or dramatic action. In the Middle Ages Scripture stories were most popular for dramatic representations, and they undoubtedly were the basis of the oratorio as we have it to-day. In the fourteenth century the choristers of St. Paul regularly performed certain miracle plays, as they were called, in which were fine choruses and some single part songs, but between that century and the sixteenth very little progress seems to have been made in them. In the year 1600 both the oratorio and the opera were presented in Italy, but as in every other form of composition a great many changes were made, many new ideas evolved and elaborated before Handel in the "Messiah" fairly perfected the scheme of composition. An Italian composer named Emilio del Cavaliere was the first composer of an oratorio, but the musical interest of the day in Italy inclined so strongly to operatic music that Cavaliere did not follow his first attempt with anything as remarkable. Handel, however, seizing upon such suggestions as the Italians of the centuries preceding had offered, and building largely on the old forms of mediæval sacred plays, produced his oratorios as you have seen, with a success which time has not diminished. It is said that should the student be chiefly interested in the study of the historical oratorio, an Italian composition of Handel's, "La Resurrezione," will afford the best example. When Handel wrote it the oratorio had kept up, so to speak, in development with the opera—by which I mean that they were treated in point of composition, arias, and arrangement of melody very nearly in the same way—but when they received the German spirit, something more solemn and dignified resulted. Finally, when that tempestuous, tumultuous, inspired fortnight occurred in Handel's life, in the year 1741, during which time he composed the "Messiah," we may consider the oratorio as perfected. Up to that point choral writing was not based on any especially stated rules. Handel was free to do with it what he liked; he had the inspiring words of the Scripture to guide him in the composition of choruses such as never had been listened to before. The orchestra of his day, although different from ours, was a fine one, and well suited to Handel's purpose, and in all airs which belong to what is known as the Cantabile kind he had artistic sense enough to do away as much as possible with an orchestral accompaniment, for which reason the finest singers are always glad of an opportunity to display their powers and express their highest musical feelings in works like the "Judas" or the "Messiah." No greater evidence of the effect of personal feeling in composition can be given than in the "Messiah." Handel's whole soul was in the work. When he was writing the exquisitely pathetic and beautiful movement beginning, "He was despised," the composer was thoroughly overcome and burst into tears, and it is related that he spent part of the day playing and reading such portions of the Testament as belong to the Passion of our Lord. When composing the beautiful introduction to "Comfort ye my people," Handel declared that the constantly repeated major chords which follow the tender, lingering, minor cadences in the overture, spoke to him directly words of comfort, and so precisely expressed what he most desired to convey — an impression of the saving power which Christ's message of consolation was to possess. Take the score of the "Messiah" after hearing it and go over certain special portions; trace out so far as you can the different keys employed, the various striking changes; see how wonderfully words and music are made to fit; try to read it going step by step from the opening movement to the last grand "Amen" which, when Handel had written, it is said, he uttered to himself upon his knees.

Other composers of whom we may speak later composed famous oratorios, but for grandeur and simplicity none ever written has exceeded Handel's "Messiah."

CHAPTER VII.

The Story of the Opera.—Count Vernio and his Friends.—A Musical Centre in Florence.—The First Opera.—Instruments used.—Allesandro Scarlatti.—Stradella.—The Size of the Opera in England.—Henry Purcell and the Westminster Boys.— An Old Picture.— Gluck and Marie Antoinette.—Gluck's Boyhood.—Fashion and Art.—Gluck determined to Reform the Spirit of the Opera.—Classical Music, and how to Define it.

ONE evening towards the close of the sixteenth century, a number of gentlemen were hurrying up the staircase and along the corridors of a house in Florence. They were richly dressed according to the custom of the time, but they were all students, all deeply absorbed in music, and they were on their way to the salon of one Giovanni Bardi, Conte di Vernio, for the purpose of discussing a new idea in their beloved art. Now, if we followed these gentlemen, what should we hear and see? Something very interesting, yet, from our point of view to-day, very strange. They were determined to develop *opera*, yet they had only the vaguest idea how it should be done.

The opera as we have it at present had so far been unheard of, and the only suggestion these Italian gentlemen had for such a form of musical composition was that given them by the Greek lyrical dramas in the famous theatre of ancient Athens, where plays were given accompanied by an orchestra of lyres and flutes. When the "Agamemnon" was performed every word of the dialogue was declaimed as musically as possible, and the choruses were sung as well as was possible at that time. In early English times music, or recitative, was introduced into the simplest plays usually performed in the public streets. People in various countries had been gifted with some perception of the beauty in combining music and dialogue, but, as I have said, the regular opera was unknown up to the sixteenth century.

Our Italian gentlemen discussed their new ideas over and over again before they made definite efforts to put them into practice. One of the party named Caccini wrote a series of songs, or "pieces," which he sang at Bardi's house one evening, accompanying himself on the lute. He had a beautiful voice, and delighted every one, so that his suggestion of attaching to these songs something dramatic in the way of action was received with pleasure. Little by little the idea of a musical drama gathered strength, and one of the first actual performances of which we read was at Mantua in 1594, when a work called "L'Amfi parnasso" was given. We who have heard the opera in its perfection would be, no doubt, greatly amused could we witness "L'Amfi parnasso" given precisely as it was in Italy towards the close of that splendid and warmly colored and suggestive century.

There was no overture and no instrumental accompaniment of any kind; five singers only took part in it. When two were on the stage the remaining three stood behind the scenes singing a kind of accompaniment. Everybody in Mantua was charmed by this performance, considered entirely novel and very graceful in character, but what would dear old Master Vecchio, who wrote it, have said had he looked ahead nearly three hundred years to the time of the great Bayreuth festival, where Wagner's operas were produced with such a wealth of orchestration and so many glorious and superbly trained voices?

Conte Vernio's house was not the only one in Florence where the new musical impulse was well received and helped on. A nobleman named Corsi received the musicians of the day, offering them every encouragement, and especially urging on the work of one Jacopo Peri and Vincent Galileo —father of the great astronomer—and Caccini. These three young men were burning with genius, and possessed a great amount of energy, but it appears that no one of the three had much knowledge of harmony or counterpoint. Caccini, as I have told you, wrote a series of very dramatic songs, or, as they were called, canzonettes, which were the basis of music of a more dramatic character. The special importance of this music to the student of to-day lies in the fact that it was the first written for a single voice, the first composed for an accompaniment of one instrument, and, as may be imagined, it produced a marked effect upon music, both vocal and instrumental, all over the world. Madrigals had preceded these canzonettes, and no doubt contained much more that was more pleasing to the ear than many of the new songs offered the public by the composers of the latter part of the sixteenth and the beginning of the seventeenth century; but there is no doubt that we owe to the three musicians I have mentioned the first definite idea for the music known technically as Monodia, which is a term from the Greek, single, a song, "and applied by modern critics to music written in what is sometimes called the homophonic style; that is to say, music in which the melody is confined to a single part instead of being equally distributed between all the voices employed, as in the polyphonic schools."*

Peri, at the suggestion of Signor Corsi, wrote a work in the operatic style called "Dafne," "in order," as he says himself, "to test the effect of the particular kind of melody which they imagined to be identical with that used by the ancient Greeks and Romans throughout their dramas, and"

---

* Grove's Musical Dictionary, page 354.

although we are told that "it charmed the whole city" of Florence, where it was performed, it was not sufficiently characteristic to create a school of similar composition. I think it safe to say that the first true Italian opera, on which all of ours have been founded, was Peri's next work, "Eurydice," which he composed in honor of the marriage of King Henry IV. of France with Maria of Medici. The performance of this opera—the first ever given in public—took place in the year 1600, and raised the whole of Italy to enthusiasm. The libretto was written by Rinaccini, and the noblemen of Florence contended for the honor of performing in it. Behind the scenes Corsi, the liberal patron of the Florentine art, presided at the harpsichord, while three noted men of Florence performed on the chitarone, a very long, deeply-necked lute, with wire strings and two sets of tuning-pegs (an old chitarone is preserved in the South Kensington Museum), a viol, and a large lute. Three flutes were added to this little orchestra. In the library of the British Museum is a copy of the score of this opera, which, when I read it, seemed to me to possess much delicacy and spirit, and I believe that good critics consider it a work of decided art in spite of Peri's ignorance of many of the rules of counterpoint.

From this hour the opera was recognized as a form of art in musical composition, and as the interest in music, espe-

THE BOY LULLI.

cially where a dramatic spirit could be added, was beginning to be felt all over Europe, it progressed and developed rapidly, as you may imagine.

It would be impossible in this space to tell you the story of the opera in detail—how it advanced steadily, in France reaching a great height, where a composer named Lulli, in 1650, established it among the French people. Lulli had been brought from Florence as a page in the court of Louis XIV. He served the king's niece, Mademoiselle de Montpensier, and no doubt he had listened from boyhood to all the finest music of the day in her boudoir.

Among Italian composers of this early period the man who seems to me most interesting was Alessandro Scarlatti. He made striking improvements in the form of the opera, varied its monotony in many original ways, and, best of all, insisted upon its being written from a scientific point of view. Peri and his followers had not cared particularly for writing according to the strict rules of harmony. They seemed to have despised the art of counterpoint, and therefore it is that their work could never live, or do more than please the uneducated ear. Our debt of gratitude to them is for their discovery, as it were, of what could be done with music and dialogue, and their zeal in carrying out an entirely novel method, but to Scarlatti we owe the bringing of science to bear upon this first brilliant suggestion.

Stradella, a famous contemporary of Scarlatti, wrote in the operatic style, and at the same time contributed largely to church music in his day, giving to it a peculiar character, a certain breadth and melodious form, different from the more solemn strains of church composers who had preceded him. Stradella's life was a very sad one, ending tragically. He was a gentleman of great refinement, but not of high rank, so that when he became engaged to one of his pupils whose rank was far above his own it created a great deal of excitement in Florence and Venice. Stradella and his fair pupil were married, and would have lived very happily but for the fact that assassins constantly pursued him. Once three of these men tried to kill him. They followed him to the church of St. John in Rome, where he was to sing, but there, while listening to his heavenly voice, their purpose changed; his music dissipated all their blood-thirsty feelings, and they made their escape, afraid to confront their employers with stainless hands. Stradella, however, was not destined to escape the vengeance of his wife's friends. In Genoa both husband and wife were secretly stabbed to death, no trace of the assassins being found.

Of the rise and progress of the opera in England much could be said, but I must group only a few facts about some one centre.

The English seem from very early times to have de-

IN THE CHOIR-SCHOOL AT WESTMINSTER ABBEY.

lighted in combining music with a certain sort of dialogue. It was the custom, as I have said, to give performances in the public streets, the singers standing in large carts, around which crowds of people collected. With all their grotesqueness and absurdity there was a dignity about them which impressed their rude audiences.

In 1658 was born in London a boy named Henry Purcell. Music seemed to grow with him. When he was very young he was put into the choir school at Westminster Abbey, and it was only the other day I was standing in the old school-room where the boy Purcell sat, and looking at a quaint old picture of him which hangs upon the wall.

The Westminster boys were taught music very fairly by old Cook and Humphries. It must have been a cheerful life. To-day the school has been enlarged and beautified, but even then it surely possessed the charm of peace, and yet great harmonies, for it stands almost in the shelter of the abbey, and all day long the boys had the dear old cloister to run about in, and twice a day they listened to glorious music on the organ. Purcell grew full of musical fire, and when he was eighteen he was appointed organist of the great abbey. He wrote constantly, catches, glees, songs, and hymns, which to this day are listened to and sung with delight.

It was when Purcell was about nineteen that he one day

received an invitation from a school-master to call, on musical business, at his house in Chelsea. Thither he went. He found a young ladies' school, and an energetic master who wished his pupils to perform something operatic. So Purcell wrote the music, and Tate the words, of "Dido and Æneas," a little operetta in which he himself performed, and which was so successful that henceforth he wrote chiefly for the stage.

But all the time everybody in London was singing or playing his glees and madrigals. In Westminster was a famous old tavern known as Purcell's Head, and clubs used to meet there to sing his music. Meanwhile we can fancy Milton as a youth playing his most solemn music in that quaint room of his, with its faded hangings and grand organ, and at the theatre elaborate performances of "The Tempest," "The Indian Queen," and other plays, to which was added "Mr. Purcell's musicke."

Those were rollicking and riotous times. Purcell's sweet music seems to come in with some feeling of soothing sounds, but had the times been better he would have done more, I am sure, in his noblest direction. Everything at court and around it was careless and reckless. Dryden, the poet, who wrote many of the plays for which Purcell furnished the music, bitterly regretted when he was older that he had wasted so much time amusing an ungodly people.

Purcell seems only to have thought of his music, and certainly at this date, two hundred years after his death, his sweetness and charm are as strongly felt. In 1695 he died, and his tomb is in the abbey where his childish feet so often passed and repassed, and beneath the organ where he so often played in his most innocent and most happy years.

When I was a child I used to be very fond of a faded little picture which I often saw in an old lady's house. It hung on a staircase, and going up and down I liked to stop and look at it, and make up stories about the two people in it. The picture represented a fine room, evidently in a palace. A splendidly dressed young lady, with a tremendous coiffure and a brocaded gown, was seated before a spinet or old-fashioned piano. Just behind her was a gentleman, also dressed in the fashion of 1770. He seemed to be teaching her to play. The young lady, I thought, was charmingly pretty. The gentleman had a strong, rather stern face, high cheek bones, and a large forehead, but the look of his eyes was not unkindly. Underneath the picture was printed in script, with a great many flourishes,

"*Gluck and Marie Antoinette.*"

The little picture was of no special merit as a work of art, yet it possessed such an extraordinary fascination for my childish eyes that the other day, when at a concert I listened to some of Gluck's sweetest music, the strains seemed to bring it back in a flash to my mind's eye. In imagination I again saw clearly the little ebony frame and faded tints, the pretty, smiling young dauphiness, and the grave though kind-hearted master.

That scene was but one from the life of Gluck, who was famous in the last century for his operas, his social popularity, his grand pupils, and last, but what is best of all, his being the founder of opera in its most classical form.

On July 2, 1714, Christoph Willibald Ritter von Gluck was born at Weidenwang. His father was in the service of a prince, and Christoph had all the musical advantages of the period, specially those of the Jesuit College at Kommotau, where he learned to sing, to play the harpsichord and the organ and the violin. He early tried his hand at composition; his ideas were mainly dramatic, but the opera of that day was not satisfactory, and you must bear in mind, when criticising Gluck's early work, that orchestral music, except in a very few places, was not understood, and at least the arrangement of the orchestra as we have it now was not known, and as a rule conductors of the theatre or concert band played on the harpsichord, keeping time not too well, for a few instruments which were imperfectly put together and with but little idea of harmony. Chamber music consisted chiefly of trios, the quartette not then be-

PAPA HAYDN.

ing in use, and anything distinctly like a classical composition in the operatic or dramatic style had not been offered to the public. Italian music had spread its influence over the northern countries of Europe, but before Gluck's day Bach and Handel had created something that was more decidedly German, both in sacred and secular music, and Gluck himself had strongly German instincts although he studied in Milan, and before he was of age had written and produced eight operas in the Italian style.

These were not a great advance on those of other writers, but Gluck felt quite sure that something much better could be done, and when in 1736 he went to England, he visited Handel, who was then prosperous and busy in the court of George II.

Gluck was only twenty-two, an eager, restless young man, with his head full of ideas, and a pocket full of manuscripts. To old Handel he showed his music and begged for criticism, but Handel would only admit that it "promised well." But he gave Gluck a most valuable suggestion when he declared that the young composer of the operas should turn his attention to counterpoint, to something which would result in a more masterly style. Off went Gluck to Paris, and there meeting with much encouragement from the poets and writers of the day, as well as the royal family, set to work on a new basis.

The opera, as it was then written, consisted simply of a series of songs in which the story of the opera was related; there were some imperfectly rendered recitations, an orchestral accompaniment was unskilfully devised, and, as a rule, worse performed, but the airs were frequently very popular, and the whole thing was kept going because it pleased the public taste. The instinct of genius, however, could not be satisfied by any work planned and produced on so irregular and incorrect a model, and Gluck decided that he could and would reform operatic composition. In France he obtained suggestions of a fine style of dramatic recitative; in Italy his natural taste for melody had been cultivated, and his experience in England and in Germany taught him the use of a carefully arranged orchestra.

In one of his letters, translated by Lady Wallace, he writes: "My purpose was to restrict music to its true office, that of ministering to the expression of poetry without interrupting the action."

Fashion governed art and music very curiously in those days. It was in 1746 that there was a rage in England for what was called the "glasses." This was in reality a harmonica—an instrument made of glasses, and which, by applying a finger moistened with water, produced what were considered agreeable concords. It is odd to think of the great composer Gluck making his bow before the public at the Haymarket Theatre, as a performer on the musical glasses. In one of Horace Walpole's famous letters, he writes of this event as stirring the fashionable world. The instrument later became very popular, and Mozart and Beethoven did not disdain to write music for it.

Gluck's work went on very steadily, in spite of the controversies of his friends and enemies and his personal annoyances. Final success came with his grand opera founded on the mythological story of Orpheus and Eurydice.

I have told you that Gluck reformed the style of the opera. He modelled his work upon the old Greek ideas of dramatic art. He felt that so far the opera had been more like a concert—a mere collection of melodies and ballads; he bent all his energies to making a lyric drama of operas, and he succeeded.

In Vienna much of his time and his work had to be given to the princes and princesses, who were his patrons. On one occasion the royal family performed his opera of "Il Parnasso." About this time he taught the archduchess Marie Antoinette, and later she wrote from Paris to her sister, speaking of him as "*notre cher Gluck*" (our dear Gluck).

It was Gluck who first introduced cymbals and the big drum into the orchestra. He fought hard over this innovation. His enemies got out satirical pamphlets, in which his "big noises" were ridiculed, but Gluck went his own way, determined to carry his point and prove himself right. Gluck's last opera was "Echo et Narcisse." This was produced in 1779, and soon after he retired to Vienna, where he passed his last years among the kindest friends. In 1787 he died suddenly.

The great object of Gluck's life was attained. He made himself felt in every branch of operatic performance; he improved the method, arrangement, and especially its dramatic power; he made it a drama, and its music classical.

This word classical, as applied to music, I am sure many of our young people do not fully understand. To define it completely would be difficult, but I will try and give you some idea of what it means.

To be strictly *classical* a musical composition must be written according to the standard rules of the art, and with a *subject* or *theme* worthy of the setting. It may be very simple, it may have but slight elaboration, yet it must contain the elements of true musical inspiration and of musical art before it is *classical*. To form any correct judgment as to what is classically good, you must have some knowledge of the laws of music, so that you see how useful is the study of a certain amount of harmony to those who never aspire to fine performance. You may ask who is to judge for us whether the subject of a musical work is worthy? This has to be decided by the good taste of the person who is criticising, and at the same time we can follow the opinion of the majority of those critics whom the world allows are best fitted to form such judgments for us. Our likes and dislikes, of course, need not be governed by this, nor need music be heavy or labored to be considered "classical," as so many young people suppose. The airiest of Bach's gavottes, the most emotional of Beethoven's andantes, the most brilliant of Mendelssohn's overtures—all of these are as purely classical as the most ponderous and sublime of symphonies or sonatas. It is doing a good theme perfect justice which makes a work classical, and a poor subject, incorrectly treated, is *not* to be called music, no matter how much "dash" or "go" or so-called prettiness it may have about it; and the young student of music ought to be as careful in regard to the choice of his or her studies as in speaking of a language. To be *classical* is simply to be grammatical. Would you wish to recite a piece of poetry in a foreign tongue, without any regard to rhythm, rhyme, or reason, simply because the mere *words* in French or German were spoken? Would not such a performance seem positively ludicrous? When you can bring to your musical study the same sensitiveness and appreciation with which you regard the study of a language, you will find that you care only for what is the best, or, in other words, the *classical*.

CHAPTER VIII.

"Papa Haydn."—What came of a Frolic.—The Wig-maker's House hold.—The Wandering Minstrels.—"Whose Music is that?"—Symphonies.—What they are.—Haydn's Last Hours.

ONE day, nearly one hundred and fifty years ago, two elderly gentlemen were dining together in an old house in Hamburg, Germany; they were music-masters of note in those days. Herr Franck was the host; the guest was Herr Reuter, capellmeister at Vienna. Their conversation naturally enough was upon music, the new and the old musicians, singers and conductors. Suddenly Herr Franck declared that he had in his house a prodigy, a boy of nine years of age, whom he had brought up from the country. He had discovered him in his father's house, singing and keeping perfect time with two pieces of stick, while his father, a coach-maker, and his mother accompanied him, the one with the harp, the other with a vigorous but not untuneful voice. The Hamburg musician, detecting the possibilities of something very fine in the child's voice, as he sat there singing in the little cottage kitchen, brought him to Hamburg, where, with a fair share of blows and

YOUNG HAYDN SINGING BEFORE THE TWO GREAT MUSICIANS

scoldings, he was teaching him the divine art of music. Herr Reuter was delighted by his host's account of the little genius. The boy was summoned from the kitchen where he was dining with the cook, and no doubt enjoying his Sunday pudding with great relish, for he worked hard and did not fare too well.

I like to think of that picture—of the old wainscoted dining-room, the grave musicians looking up from their dinner as the door opens on a small, dark-haired, brown-skinned boy, a dainty, delicately modelled child, who enters shyly and stands at a distance from the table, his hands behind him and the head bent down, until his teacher, Herr Franck, bids him sing. Then the boy's voice breaks all the bonds of restraint; back goes his little head and he sings. It is an irrepressible burst of melody; up springs Reuter, the old master, exclaiming, "He shall come to my choir; he is just what I want."

This was a wonderful step onward for the child. But Reuter little knew the future of the boy whom he took that day, and never dreamed that his name, Francis Joseph Haydn, would be famous two centuries later in every civilized country of the world, and best known as that of the founder of the modern symphony.

Reuter carried young Haydn off to Vienna, where he was placed in the cathedral choir, and where his sweet young voice, a marvellous soprano, filled all the town with delight. His parents gave him freely in charge to old Reuter. But the master was selfish and exacting. The boy longed to compose, but Reuter refused to allow him to take lessons in composition, and made him give his whole time to choir practice. Haydn had very little money, but he hoarded every penny for a long time, and when he was thirteen years old he purchased two treatises on music, and having studied them diligently, actually composed a mass.

I do not suppose it was very fine music, but at all events it showed a great desire for work, and it was too bad that Reuter should have roared with laughter over it, and given the eager boy no encouragement. It seems as though from that time the old master was determined to thwart and annoy his pupil. The lad found choir-work a slavery, but did not know how to free himself. A piece of idle mischief led to his escape. One day in a frolic he cut off the tail of the wig of a singer in the choir. Reuter flew into a rage, turning Haydn out then and there, actually expelling him from choir, board, and lodging. It was a cruel winter's night. The lad wandered about the streets of Vienna, until he remembered the one person who had ever encouraged him. This was a barber named Keller, and to his humble abode Haydn directed his steps. Keller gave him a cordial welcome, though he had but little to offer: a loft

—in which, however, stood an old harpsichord—and a seat at his simple table. In the wig-maker's family Haydn went joyfully to work. He had some sonatas of Bach's, he picked up odd bits of music here and there, mastered the science of those who had gone before him, and though often cold and hungry, was never cheerless. Now and then he went into the shop, where Keller and his daughter Anne were at work on wigs, and where Haydn's assistance was quite acceptable. Anne Keller was a plain, dull girl, who knew nothing of the great art of her father's lodger, yet Haydn was grateful for her rough sort of kindness to him. He became engaged to her, and later, when he was more prosperous, married her.

It was not long before the young musician had made a circle of friends. He played on the violin and the organ, sometimes in the churches and occasionally in the salons of some great ladies, but his chief enjoyment was a little club of wandering minstrels. They were a band of enthusiastic youths who wandered about Vienna on moonlight nights to serenade famous musicians.

One night they directed their steps to the house of Herr Curtz, the leader of the Opera. Under his windows they began one of Haydn's compositions, the young musician's violin slowly filling the moonlit garden with melody. No demonstration from old Curtz was expected, but suddenly a window was flung open, out came Curtz's head, and his voice screamed to know who was playing.

Back came the answer, "Joseph Haydn."

"Whose music is it?"

"Mine."

Down came Curtz, collared the astonished young man, and brought him up-stairs to a big, candle-lit room, where stood a fine piano littered with music. There, when the two had regained their breath, Curtz explained that he wanted Haydn to compose some music for a new libretto he had written. Now this was certainly an important moment. Haydn sat down to the piano, banged away, tried various ideas, and at last hit upon the right thing. Before daylight he had arranged with Curtz for the music, for which he was promised one hundred and thirty florins.

It was his first real success, and from that moment prosperity attended him. He wrote his first symphony when he was twenty-eight, in the year 1759. Soon after he received an appointment in the household of Prince Esterhazy, where his duty was a curious one. He was obliged to have a piece of music ready to lay on his patron's breakfast-table every morning. This may seem drudgery, but in reality these years were among the happiest of Haydn's life, marred only by his marriage with the barber's daughter, Anne Keller, whose wretched temper at last forced him to separate from her. He cared for her tenderly, however, and she was well content with her lot in life.

Around Haydn, in England, France, and Germany, a band of young musicians gathered, eager to watch his developments in music. Among them Mozart, then a very youthful composer, was not only the greatest genius but the most interesting figure. He it was who gave to the master that endearing title of "Papa Haydn," whereby he was and even now is tenderly and familiarly known. Between the two men existed the most touching friendship, broken only by Mozart's early death.

I have told you that Haydn was the founder of the symphony as we know it to-day. Strictly speaking, the symphony is a long and elaborate composition for a full orchestra; arranged for a piano it suggested wind and stringed instruments, and if properly played gives a fine idea of all the orchestral effects produced. Any number of instruments may be employed in its execution, and voices are occasionally added. The movements of the symphony are four: the *allegro*, the *andante* or *adagio*, the *minuet* or *scherzo*, and the *allegro* or *presto*. Two themes or subjects, or we might say ideas, are employed in the first movement, and these are given in two different keys, the theme working back and forth, up and down, returning to the original key with grace or strength or brilliancy, or it may be a pathos which belongs to certain progressions from the minor to the major and *vice versa*. Once the symphony was started, it, as you may readily imagine, suggested innumerable improvements in the orchestra of the day; consequently Haydn's work was not alone that of composition, but of development for musicians in different ranks, and when finally produced, his work created by its demands a supply of good material in the orchestra which was speedily forthcoming.

Not alone upon the symphony did Haydn work. His oratorio, "The Creation," was composed in 1799, and his quartettes and concertos are of a superior order.

With a performance of "The Creation" in 1809 is associated one of the last scenes of Haydn's life.

The public of Vienna wished to pay their honored musician a tribute, and so the oratorio was given with every possible brilliancy of effect and performance. Haydn was an old man, and very feeble, and he was obliged to be carried into the theatre; but there he sat near his dear friend Princess Esterhazy, while all eyes turned lovingly and reverently towards him.

When the music reached that part in which the words "Let there be light" occur, Haydn rose, and pointing heavenward said, aloud, "It comes from thence;" and indeed all knew that the master's work was always a subject of prayer and humble supplication that he might be able to do the best for the good of all.

After that evening Haydn never left his house. He grew feebler daily, but suffered little pain. One day, when he was thought to be past consciousness, he suddenly rose from his couch, and by a superhuman effort reached the piano.

There, in a voice which yet held the cadences of the boy chorister of long ago, he sang the national hymn, and so, his hands dropping on the keys, he was carried gently to his bed and to his peaceful death. This was in May, 1809: Francis Joseph Haydn, born in 1732, died in his seventy-eighth year.

CHAPTER IX.

The Story of the Sonata.—Suites and Madrigals.—Corelli's Work.—Anecdote of Handel in Rome.—"C Major."—The Movements of the Sonata Explained and Defined.—Old Dances and Dance Tunes.—What the Minstrels and Soldiers of the Sixteenth Century Introduced.—Minuets.—Scherzos.

THE history of the sonata is one which I am sure all young students who enjoy their work could read in detail with both profit and much entertainment, for it belongs to a most picturesque and interesting period in musical art. At the end of the sixteenth century a great desire arose among musical enthusiasts to create some form of music which would express feelings of various kinds. Up to that time the grandest form of composition had been used only in church-music, and while these earnest individuals had no desire to detract from the power and beauty of such music, they considered rightly enough that a refining influence in society would be music which appealed more to their human sentiments than those inspired only by the solemnity of religious ceremonial. The opera and the cantata had been received, and although by no means perfect were successful; but an elaborate form of composition such as became known later under the name of *sonata* was not known until the end of the sixteenth century. Even then such pieces were much more simple than the sonata as we see it one hundred and fifty years later; the sonata, indeed, which Beethoven finally perfected and handed down to us. Originally, about 1620, the sonata consisted of but one movement, and seems to have come from the madrigals of that period. What were called *suites* often formed a suggestion for those early sonatas, for which reason we find that the names applied to different parts of such a work closely resemble those used for the dance tunes of the sixteenth and seventeenth centuries. When written for church-music, as it was in that day, the sonata consisted of slow, solemn movements, but the sonata as we have it to-day must consist of four movements. The drama also suggested some of the musical ideas used in its formation, and there is no doubt that it at one time was used as an accompaniment for vocal performance. Were it possible to go into close detail, I could give you a score of names connected with early sonatas and many stories belonging to their time; but what we have to consider is the sonata as we have it to-day. Perhaps the sonatas of a musician named Corelli may be considered as a fair starting-point, since he worked with a close regard to forms and published sixty sonatas of different kinds, chiefly beginning with a slow movement, very dignified and stately, and followed by three movements of varied character. Corelli was born in Fusignano, in Italy, in 1653. He studied counterpoint or such harmony and thorough-bass as could then be taught from Simonelli and the violin from Basani. On this instrument he is said to have performed marvellously well, but an anecdote related of him and Handel indicates somewhat the delicacy but lack of vigor in his style. Handel was in Rome for the purpose of conducting some of his own cantatas. A *cantata* is a kind of short opera or oratorio, and was originally a sort of musical recitation by a person with no dramatic performance and accompanied by one instrument; at present it consists of a choral work of more elaborate character; too short to be called an oratorio, and when it is secular too light in tone or melody to be dignified by that name. Handel's cantatas were many of them very stately and grand, and in the special one which he directed in Rome while Corelli led the band there occur some very powerful passages. Corelli, as well as being leader of the band, played first violin; and exquisite as was his style Handel lost all patience over the tame way in which he produced these parts, especially where the following notes occur.

CHRISTOPH RITTER VON GLUCK.

At last, unable to endure it any longer, Handel rushed forward and snatched the violin out of Corelli's hands, stamping up and down before him, began to fairly thunder it forth, singing loudly and playing on the instrument at the same time. Corelli listened, answered most politely some of Handel's violent remarks and calmly began over again, not even losing his temper, but not giving the passage in question with any more vigor, for which reason Handel never could be brought to do Corelli justice as a composer or performer, but he is well known now to have reformed many points in *technique;* and limited as he was both in composition and performance, we owe him a great deal for his methodical manner and his patience in rearranging the confused ideas which belonged to that period. Sometimes he made startling mistakes, one of which indicates the lack of musical knowledge at that day, and being connected with the famous composer Scarlatti is especially interesting. The two composers were at a concert for the King of Naples. Corelli was leading, and in a composition of Scarlatti's made some small mistakes which confused him in spite of Scarlatti's efforts to gloss it over. The next piece was in the key of C minor. Corelli began it in C major. "We will begin again," whispered Scarlatti, but again and again Corelli failed to see or to rectify his mistake; and it is said that so great was his humiliation that his health immediately began to fail, and in fact he died soon afterwards, in January, 1713.

The four movements of the sonata are as follows: first an *allegro*, next an *andante*, following this a *minuet* or *scherzo* —this was introduced by Beethoven—the fourth movement again *allegro* or *presto* or *rondo*. The allegro has two of what are called themes or subjects, one in the tonic or key-note, the other in the dominant. This is the fifth note above the key-note; for example, should the first theme of an allegro be written in C, the second would have to be in G. It is called the dominant because the key to any passage cannot be actually known unless it has this note for the root. Should the first theme of the sonata be written in the minor key then the second would have to be in the relative major.

The second movement of the sonata, the andante, has usually one theme or subject, and it is a key which relates in some way to the tonic or leading key. The third movement, the minuet, has its origin in music of French origin. It was written always in dancing time. Sometimes it is called the trio, because of its second movement being composed in three part harmony. When we come to consider the symphony we will hear more of the minuet and scherzo time. The fourth movement goes back to the original key, but there is only one theme, and this is often repeated over and over in various ways.

This, of course, is merely an outline whereby composers have a certain rule to govern them, but they are allowed certain license, so that occasionally you will find sonatas written without close adherence to this form. Schubert constantly disregarded rules in his sonatas, and occasionally Beethoven did the same. To Haydn, Mozart, and Beethoven we owe the sonata as we have it now; for beginners I should recommend Haydn and Mozart as the simplest reading and best music to begin upon.

The actual meaning of the term *allegro* is "cheerful," from which you can form some idea of its application in musical expression, but its proper significance relates to the speed to be used in playing any portion of a piece of music which is marked allegro. The tempo of such portions is between andante and presto. Various words are combined with allegro, such as "molto," "conbrio," which indicate a quickening of the time; then the "allegro moderato," or "non troppo," meaning a slower time; while the size of the hall in which an orchestra are playing, the number of performers, and many such points indicate the time in which the allegro is to be taken, no matter how the marks read on the music.

The andante, following the allegro in a sonata, means to "move along at a moderate pace," and like *adagio* and *largo* the term is used as a name for a piece of music, or else as the name for one movement *always* taken slowly in sonata, symphony, etc.

The minuet or scherzo, which is the third movement of the sonata, was introduced by Beethoven. The minuet is a piece of music in dancing measure, and is emphatically of French origin. The name is from *menu,* and refers to the small steps of the dance. When it was invented is uncertain. A French composer named Lulli is supposed by many to have invented it. The first form of the minuet consisted of two eight-bar phrases in ¾ time. These were repeated, sometimes beginning on the third beat of the bar, but generally upon the first, and the movement was extremely moderate and precise.

Mozart, in "Don Giovanni," has written what is considered the most perfect form of the original minuet. Following this first movement came a second written in three-part harmony, for which reason it was called a *trio.* Frequently the second part of the dance contained sixteen or more bars in place of the original eight. In what is known as the *suite* we frequently find a minuet in this form. The suites which led the way to the sonata were a collection of dance tunes, and their history is interesting, romantic, and picturesque. In the latter part of the sixteenth, and in the beginning of the eighteenth century, dancing tunes had spread all over civilized Europe. Travelling musicians took them from place to place entertaining the ladies and gentlemen of Court with them, while people returning from the wars or soldiers of foreign nations brought from place to place the dances characteristic of their own climes; and the French and German and English people adopted them, in course of time popularizing them as completely as though they had originated among themselves.

In Queen Elizabeth's day there was music of various kinds ordained for dancing. Suites consisting of "*A staid musicke ordered for grave dancing,*" and again a "*lighter and more stirring kind.*" The poets of her day make frequent references to these old dancing tunes, which are significant to us now in our study of sonata or symphony, as germs of the original feeling remain enough in both tempo and treatment to be suggestive, or to create a background for us as we practise, which makes work for us both picturesque and entertaining. The variety in styles and methods of dancing and dancing tunes suggested the idea of putting together a collection, in which there should be a sufficient contrast to make the performance amusing and inspiring. Therefrom started the suite. Dances of various countries were selected, and composers of genius and note devoted much time to working for them.

The dances, of course, are too numerous to mention—*Pavans*, *Galliards*, *Allemanes*, and *Branles* originated in

Italy, Suabia, and France—and when these passed out of fashion the *Allemandes* and *Courantes* and the *Sarabande* came into favor. Following these the *Minuet*, the *Riygadoon*, the *Chacone*, and finally in the English suite the *Jig* appeared. A description of these dances is not necessary here, although their characteristic would be well worthy of study to the pianist, because of their direct influence upon music and the suggestions which they offer for expression and feeling, as well as for the impetus which the history of any part of a science is sure to give to the study of it. The *scherzo*, from the Italian word meaning jest, belongs to the sonata, and occupies a prominent position therein. The old minuet or trio formed the groundwork of the scherzo as Beethoven developed it, and in it certain phrases are repeated, introduced and reintroduced with endless variations in a spirit of gayety and musical mirth which are charming when in the hands of a great composer. The movement is short, the rhythm carefully marked, and triple time considered the best. Sometimes for the sake of strong contrast different time is used, but Beethoven clung, whenever it was possible, to the $\frac{3}{4}$ time, even when another tempo might have been as well used. An admirable critic—Professor Gehring of Vienna—suggests that this has been done so that the written notes should attract the eye and therefore impress the mind of the player with the composer's idea of a "tripping lightness"—a quick rhythm, the three notes with their little "separated stems" being more suggestive than quavers with united ends. In Beethoven's C minor symphony the scherzo is worthy of the closest attention: suddenly it rushes from gayety into something terror-stricken and pursued, returning, as the above-quoted critic says, "All alive and well,"* in the tremendously joyful finale. All sorts of eccentricities are employed in the scherzo of the 8th symphony; especially when in rushes the tremendous bass with its C sharp converted into D flat, and just as the whole thing seems to have culminated in the chord of F repeated, behold there is a fresh impetus aroused—a start up again, and a new and brilliant finale. The scherzo of the 9th symphony is considered very typical, and the phrase given below indicates the character of the whole.

Together with the study of the different portions of the sonata and the symphony, it is well to make especial note of the *keys* and their reference to each other.

---

* Professor Gehring does not suggest any resemblance in Schumann's work to this special scherzo, but it seems to me that there are strong characteristics in common.

CHAPTER X.

Wolfgang Amadeus Mozart.—"Master and Miss Mozart, Prodigies of Nature."—A Concert in the London of 1765.—"Nannerl."—The Children's Presents.—Home Discipline.—The House in Chelsea.—Playing and Composing.—The First Symphony.—An Old Letter.—Duets a Novelty.—In Italy.—The First Opera.—An Important Visit.—The Weber Family.—A Heartless Coquette.—Constanza.—"The Magic Flute."—Last Days.

In the month of May, 1765, an advertisement appeared in London, announcing that a concert would be given at Hicksford's Rooms, Brewer Street, Golden Square, "For the benefit of Miss Mozart, aged thirteen, and Master Mozart, eight years of age, prodigies of nature—a concert of music, with all the overtures of this little boy's own composition."

Suppose that we had been able to attend that concert in May, 1765. A charming occasion it must have been, for London was quite excited over the event; piano-forte performances were novel enough then, at least so far as special representations of the kind are concerned, to give this occasion a character of its own; children, "prodigies of nature," were particularly acceptable to the London public.

WOLFGANG AMADEUS MOZART.

At that time precocity among young misses and masters was regarded very favorably; we read of quite small children being brought into company for the purpose of entertaining older minds who had grown tired of the round of foolish dissipations and ordinary social pleasures; small children, scarcely able to speak their own language, sometimes recited in classic tongues; dances were devised requiring grace and accuracy, and the little people who performed them were fêted and made much of, so that the performances of Miss Mozart and her small brother were hailed with delight.

Very few of the prodigies, however, of that splendid period, lived to fulfil any promise of their childhood; but as we read or hear the sonatas of Wolfgang Amadeus Mozart to-day—as we listen to the never-tiring strains of "Don Giovanni"—as the organ swells forth in the glorious masses to which he has given his name, the scene in Golden Square rises as a background for so much that is wonderful and inspiring, that we fain would conjure up its every detail, separating it very clearly from occasions of a lighter character in those summer seasons when George III. was young and music beginning to be patronized. I am sure there was a great deal of jostling about of sedan-chairs and footmen that evening, and in the spring twilight—they gave concerts earlier then than now — the gorgeously dressed ladies and gentlemen must have looked very much like a picture. Let us follow them into Hicksford's Rooms. We find ourselves in a large and well-lighted hall with chairs and benches and a large platform containing some instruments and a good harpsichord. Out comes old Papa Mozart, a dignified gentleman from Salzburg, leading a child by each hand: one a charmingly pretty little girl in the quaint dress we are reviving to-day; the other a boy of eight, of a most striking grace and beauty, and dressed like a little court gentleman—that is, with knee-breeches, silken hose, shoebuckles, a little satin coat with lace ruffles, and a little sword at his side. The little boy makes his bow to an enthusiastic audience; he sits down at the piano, and forthwith begins one of his own sweet, childlike, yet harmonious compositions. Then "Nannerl," as she is called, plays. Presently the two young prodigies vanish, the fine audience moves away, the lights are out, and the boy's London fame had begun. As we go through dingy Golden Square to-day, one hundred and eighteen years later, we think of all the music he left for us to hear and feel and play between that night when he performed his own little compositions, and the day of his death in 1791, at the early age of thirty-five years.

Wolfgang Amadeus Mozart was born at Salzburg in 1756. His father had possessed musical talent, which descended to the boy as genius. At three years of age he learned to play; before he was five he had composed a great many little melodies, which his father wrote down for him.

I remember seeing in the studio of an English artist* in London, himself the son of a great musician, a picture representing the baby Mozart: a charming little figure leading a visionary choir of angels. It seemed to me the very embodiment of what Mozart might have been as a child—beautiful, fascinating, angelic, and a musician from his soul to his very finger-tips.

His sister Anna, or "Nannerl," as they called her at home, also played marvellously well, and when the children were very young their father started with them on a concert tour, during which time they played in London. As I told you, the great ladies and gentlemen of the day delighted in juvenile precocity; the little Mozarts were fêted and caressed in a way which would have spoiled the lad's sweet, sunny nature, perhaps, but for his father's watchful care. With the true German instinct for discipline, the elder Mozart guarded his children carefully from over-excitement or indulgence. Presents were constantly made them — garments of satin trimmed with finest of laces. Rich jewels, besides all sorts of fanciful and expensive toys, were

---

* Mr. Felix Moscheles.

showered upon the children. And even out of these the careful father found a means of training the children's natures; the clothes were used only on concert or special social occasions; the jewellery was kept locked away in a large box, and the children were only allowed to take it out and look at it when their behavior had been particularly good. They were permitted to play with it for a little while, but its intrinsic value was never told them. During this London visit the Mozarts were for a time in lodgings in Chelsea, a part of London which was then an open country, with blooming gardens and green lanes stretching in every direction, while the roar of the great city was far in the distance, and even Hicksford's Rooms were a long journey away.

Old Mr. Mozart fell ill, and for some time the children had to keep very quiet. The harpsichord was closed, and the brother and sister took to running about the pretty, suburban place, no doubt enjoying the respite from practising; but even in this happy time Mozart's little brain was at work with musical compositions. The enforced idleness and freedom from care was in its way productive. He delighted to romp with Nannerl, to build up a little house of stone and moss and weeds in the garden back of their lodgings; but undercurrent was the impulse towards musical work, mingling with his play and frolics, and finally taking definite shape, when he composed his first symphony

(Opus 15). He was then in his tenth year, but in this work an amount of scientific knowledge is displayed which, taking the resources of the time into consideration, shows us what sparkling genius the boy Mozart possessed. Soon after this the father recovered, the family removed to a quaint old inn in Cornhill, London, and more concerts were advertised; but the children had their precious souvenir of that "field-and-flower" holiday in the manuscript which was produced to the delight of the father during his convalescence, and among the novelties offered in the programme were "Duets for Four Hands on the Harpsichord."

This was in the year 1765. Among the treasures in an old house in England I have seen preserved a letter in which these performances are alluded to; one could wish that the writer had given more detail; but as would be natural, I suppose she, being the mother of two little people of her own, dwelt more on her anxiety that her children should be able to do like "Master and Miss Mozart" than upon the methods and appearance of the latter. She refers to their performance as "vastly amusing," and says that the boy has a "most engaging look," and the little girl a "sweet German face, with a very serious although enchanting expression." Still the letter shows how entirely novel and quaint a proceeding it was considered. People who crowded to hear the children desired strongly to visit them at home; and it would seem as though they almost believed there was some trickery in the way the performance was conducted, for Mozart the elder at last announced a series of "test" entertainments.

In the old inn was a large, wainscoted room where the harpsichord was placed. Here audiences including the talent, wit, and fashion of London assembled twice a week, while the children, attired in all their bravery—and perhaps on these occasions being permitted to wear some of the delightful jewellery—were brought forward, the audience being requested to "test" them at the harpsichord. It is said they never failed in satisfying and delighting their hearers, the boy charming every one by his gayety, his quaintness, his sweetness of temper, and as well the *abandon* with which he entered into his work; and Nannerl, the little, serious-eyed, blooming *mädchen*, fascinating the brilliant company by her simplicity and talent, and the adoring fondness she showed for her little brother.

Passing from this time of sunny though precocious childhood to a boyhood in which he worked indefatigably, we find Mozart in Italy, studying, composing, performing, and writing the most delightful letters home, chiefly to his dear Nannerl, who by this time was more devoted to domestic duties than music. But to her the boy always poured forth his musical sentiments. Did he hear anything which pleased him it was to Nannerl that he desired to write it; and I think in all the history of great lives there has rarely been anything more touching than the devotion displayed by Mozart to those whom he loved — first to his parents and sister, later to his wife.

One of the most interesting experiences of the Mozarts took place after the Italian visit in 1775. The Elector of Bavaria invited Mozart to write an opera for the Carnival. Mozart set to work speedily, watched over by his parents and sister, and when the work was completed—it was called "La Tinta Giardanera" — the father and son, with pretty Nannerl, set off for Munich, where court life was then very gay.

In the old market-place at Munich lived a very respectable widow, and Nannerl, a charming maiden at that time, was taken there to lodge, the father and son being compelled to be nearer court. Of course Nannerl shared all the delights and excitement of the visit. Rehearsals began at once, and young Mozart darted in and out of his sister's lodging half a dozen times a day to report progress. Not very long ago I was standing in the door-way of the old house, and looking up the heavy oaken staircase, back of a little shop, which led to the rooms where Anna Mozart spent those days; and it seemed to me that I could see Mozart's fast flying young feet as he rushed up and down, humming bits of the opera, or perhaps suggestions of the finer work which was to come later. At all events a fascinating picture, with Nannerl bending over the balustrade from the gloom of the old hall above, her sweet young face shining down a benediction upon the ardent and anxious younger brother. No musical life, unless it be that of Felix Mendelssohn, affords more charming pictures, or indeed more pathetic ones, than that of Mozart, and the sunshine in his music seems to me to belong to all this period of youth, the dawn of early manhood with which these days are so tenderly associated.

At last the grand night came. Nannerl was dressed with extremest care by the old widow, and joined her father and brother. The three were fairly trembling with excitement, Mozart slipping his fingers now and then into his sister's for a sympathetic pressure, although he carried his young head high, and in his splendid new costume of satin and lace, with the flash of diamonds in his ruff and on his slippers, looked like a young prince come forth to greet his people.

The opera-house was crowded to excess; the court was there in full splendor, and Mozart, the youthful Maestro, sat with his father and Nannerl waiting so anxiously for the performance to begin that he scarcely heeded the glances bent upon him from every side. The boy—he was scarcely nineteen—stood the blaze of admiration very well. His mind was centred upon the music, and from the first note to the last it was a triumphant success. Mozart became the object of the wildest enthusiasm, and from that hour his musical fame was established.

Unfortunately, however, all of Mozart's days were not so cloudless nor so joyful. In his short and busy life the periods of anxiety and heart-sickness seem almost to predominate, marking the serenity and the sunshine of the early days all the more clearly. The little family circle at home was so centred in the lad that when he started out on a second tour, and the father could not accompany him, the mother left her household duties to Nannerl and set forth with her son. An adoring fondness for his parents was one of the most lovely traits in Mozart's beautiful nature. On this trip he wrote home with pride how careful he was of his mother, and she, good woman, watched him tenderly, giving up everything to his pleasure and profit.

He spent the winter in Mannheim, where his letters show how very busily he was employed. He writes that he rose early, "dressed quickly," and after breakfast composed until twelve; then wrote until half-past one, when he dined. At three he began to give lessons, which continued until supper-time; after which he read, unless he was among his friends. Of course he had a large circle wherever he was, but in Mannheim during this winter he formed friendships which shadowed all his life.

The Weber family were there—brilliant musicians, agreeable and witty. There were five daughters, and Mozart straightway fell in love with the eldest, Aloysia, a beautiful girl, who was studying for the stage. She was well pleased with the young composer's attentions, and he went to Paris half, or, as he considered it, wholly engaged. That was a sad visit to Paris. His mother, wishing to economize for her son's sake, took rooms in a cold, poor quarter of the town, and there fell ill with a fatal disorder. Poor Mozart wrote home the most pathetic letters. We can fancy how he tried to save her, but it was in vain. The careful, tender, self-sacrificing mother faded from his life, her last thoughts being to commend this beloved son to God's keeping.

Full of sadness, the poor young fellow hastened to Mannheim, where he hoped Aloysia Weber would console him. She had gone to Munich, and thither he followed her. There the true selfishness of the Weber family was shown to him. They had become prosperous, and Mozart, although famous, was far from being rich, so that the family of his betrothed received him coldly. Aloysia herself scarcely listened to the first words he said. He had entered the Weber parlor full of hope and anxiety to see his future wife, and tell her the story of his sorrow. He must have looked noble and manly, with the tenderness of his grief in his handsome face, but Aloysia turned aside coldly; there were others there to whom she talked. Mozart hesitated a moment, and then seating himself at the piano, sang in his rich, clear voice, "*Ich lasse das Mädchen das nicht will*" (I leave the maiden who leaves me), and before the evening was over, the engagement was at an end.

We could wish that his intimacy with the Webers had also ended, but later he renewed acquaintance with them, and in spite of much opposition from his anxious father and Nannerl he married Constanza, Aloysia's younger sister. With her he tried to be happy, but even in his tenderest letters we see that she was ill-tempered, cold, and selfish. But Mozart's nature was so uniformly sweet that it took a great deal to make him positively wretched, and unkind he could not be.

When he was in the midst of many worries, one summer, he used to ride out every morning for exercise, and leaving his wife sleeping, he never failed to pin a little note to her pillow, that she might find it on awaking. It was always a sweet word of love and care for her, and it is hard to think Constanza was not worthy of it.

There is so much to tell of Mozart, I wish that we might linger an hour more over his sweet story. His successes were so many that it is hard to think of him as so often troubled about money.

In 1791 his beautiful opera of "The Magic Flute" was produced with tremendous success at Vienna. Constanza came on to hear it, and was thoroughly frightened by Mozart's altered looks. He was ashy pale, worn and thin. She seems to have been full of a really tender feeling for him then. He was writing his famous mass, the "Requiem," and continued it even after he took to his bed; and while Constanza sat beside him, watching with tears the feeble hand at work, he told her that his heart and soul were full of thoughts of the dear Lord who had died for him.

"The Magic Flute" was drawing crowded houses, while Mozart lay dying not far off. In the evenings he would time the performance, saying to Constanza and her sister Sophie, and some musical friends always with him, "Now they are singing this or that part." The day before his death he read over the score of the Requiem, and asked the friends near him to try and sing it with him. They did so, Mozart coming in with his part in a sweet, faint voice. Suddenly, at the *Lacrimoso*, he burst into tears, and laid down the score for the last time. That evening he murmured to Constanza, "Oh, that I could once more hear my 'Magic Flute!'"

Constanza glanced at Roser, a musician who was with them, and, blinded by his tears, Roser sat down to the piano and sang one of Mozart's favorite airs. It was almost the last sound his closing ears received. The next morning, Sunday, December 5, 1791, at the age of thirty-five, Mozart died.*

---

* Nannerl survived her brother many years. Constanza Mozart died in this century, having, in 1809, married a second time.

CHAPTER XI.

Ecclesiastical Music.—Early Writers.—Palestrina and the Council of Trent.—An Important Decision.—The Reform.—Mass Music of Various Composers.

PROBABLY no form of music has undergone so many changes as that used in Christian churches since the period of the Reformation, all kinds of local reasons producing modifications, alterations, or offering suggestions for both form and melody employed; but during the last ten years there has been in church-music a decided improvement—a strong desire to use the best forms, to employ the purest kind of melody and the most harmonious music, entirely independent of its origin or its traditional meaning. While the simple hymn tunes will always, I suppose, be more or less in vogue among the various churches, will always be beloved for sacred music at home, still the tendency is towards a finer or broader kind of harmony, something which will be worthier of study and of performance, and, at the same time, elevate the thoughts of the people, as perfectly harmonious strains of music when listened to with a fervent spirit, be it of the worship of God or the appreciation of the art itself, must always do.

At the present day all Christian churches use for their special services a great deal of what is known as old mass music; the programmes for all Easter services include so much of the music which has long been known as such, that it is well to understand the origin of what we now call the mass music in the history of the art itself; for to-day we owe to it much that is fine in all our present forms of melody, and especially a direct impulse towards an improvement in the art of singing. The history of mass music really belongs to the history of singing, but like all such phases in any art where the outgrowths are many, the actual beginning, the first causes, or the principles which dominate those beginnings, are apt to become confused or forgotten after the lapse of centuries and the constant ebb and flow of so many tides of musical feeling.

If we could look back three hundred years to Easter-time in Italy, we should see all the choir singing-schools actively at work, choir-boys running hither and thither between their hours of practice, full of enthusiasm for their work, gathering about the master with anxiety and zeal; for to sing in a choir in those days was regarded as a great favor. Not only did it open the way to musical study and advancement to any boy who showed talent, but it elevated the choir-boy, who was generally of very humble origin, and often afforded him the means of a comfortable home and some instruction.

Between the fourteenth and the seventeenth centuries, to advance in musical study it was necessary for a boy to be admitted into some choir, as all the first music belonged to the church, and was taught by the chapel-master and encouraged by the ecclesiastics. So many famous musicians and composers have devoted special periods of their lives to the composition of mass music, and, as at the present day, so much of it is employed in all Christian churches, something historical on the subject is sure to be of interest, particularly as at one time the question as to whether certain forms of music should or should not be allowed in the Roman Church produced a distinct phase in musical history which has influenced every period since that time. In the Roman Church from time immemorial the custom of singing certain parts of the mass, or church service, to music of a very impressive character has prevailed. It is difficult to say positively the exact source from which this music was derived. Tradition consecrated certain forms of melody or of chant to the service of the church, but the first collected form which we now have was revised or arranged by St. Ambrose, in the fourth century. Afterwards St. Gregory the Great continued this work. Under the name of plain chant various melodies, antique and solemn in form, are preserved, and are still constantly sung in the Pontifical Chapel of Rome, the cathedrals of most Continental dioceses, and at present in many Protestant churches, especially in the Episcopalian or Church of England.

Here is a specimen of the *Kyrie*, which is part of a mass belonging to the ninth century, and as for one thousand years after St. Gregory composed his famous chant the same characteristics are noticed here and there in all music written for church service; so that a careful observation of this early form is interesting and useful to the student.

In early times each individual portion of the mass service used to be sung to its own tune; when different church festivals occurred there were special tunes appointed for them. The invention of counterpoint, however, opened up a new field. The composers of the day were enthusiastic at once in their desire to make use of thorough-bass for mingling these tunes and other plain chant melodies into masses arranged with reference to different voices, and these in turn gave rise to those great schools of ecclesiastical music which led the way to so much that we possess to-day, that we ought to regard them with solemnity and respect.

During the latter part of the sixteenth century, the schools for ecclesiastical music gave rise to a development which has never been excelled. In the fourteenth or fifteenth century, what was called the *Canto Fermo* had been employed for mass music. This was a single, plain chant melody, or some one subject often derived from secular sources, which served as a theme for the entire mass. When composers of note who entered into the study of harmony or counterpoint began to allow their genius to take wing, the old *Canto Fermo* underwent many changes; but, fortunately, wherever in the *Canto Fermo* a fine possibility existed, or had in it anything worth preserving, the writers of sacred music treated it with proper respect.

A tenor singer in the Pontifical Chapel, about 1390, named

Du Fay, is now considered the first composer in what is called the primitive or early school of mass music. He worked hard, and his compositions are full of fine suggestions. Dunstable and Binchoys were also writers of the fourteenth century, and a singer in the Pope's chapel, who was afterwards chapel-master to Louis XII., was one of the most learned musicians of the fifteenth century. This was Josquin des Pres. His masses would be excellent specimens of ecclesiastical music but for his tendency to introduce too much that was trivial. He had an abundant genius—that is, his mind was teeming with musical suggestions—and had he lived two centuries later we should doubtless owe him a larger debt; for Des Pres needed only to have his genius rightly guided by good standards. But we must judge of people's work as much by their surroundings and resources as by the genius in the work itself, so that, looking back to the fifteenth century, we can realize how Des Pres felt at liberty to let his imagination run riot; counterpoint combined with a purely classical idea and melodic form in work had not then become fully understood. Now then, you can readily understand how, as soon as composers began to regard the plain chant as only a background for more elaborate church-music, many composers allowed themselves too much license in their sacred compositions. A reform was necessary. The result of this was, as I have suggested, one of the most important periods in the history of the art of music.

In 1564 the Council of Trent decided that it would be necessary to lay down rules for ecclesiastical music, and also to see that these should be strictly enforced and carried out. So various were the abuses which had crept into church-music, and so very difficult was it to eradicate them without making a sweeping condemnation, and laying down a strict law forbidding any but a certain kind of music, that many of the council considered it wisest to forbid any sort of what is called polyphonic music. However, many people within and without the council had become so enthusiastic over the great development in music, that some members of the council earnestly strove to oppose this measure, and suggested that it would be well to preserve as far as possible such forms of music as would include certain melody and *quartette*.

In looking back at a striking picture of that time we seem to see one figure, an outsider, yet a most impressive character—the genius, the man who determined musical history so far as church music was concerned. Going back and forth between his quiet dwelling and the chapel of St. Maria Maggiore, where he was organist during those anxious days, this musician, Palestrina by name, lived a life of thought and zealous aspiration; his brain full of musical themes and subjects which he fully believed he could work out in a manner fitting the use to which they would be put, if only the council would not lay down a law which would abolish them forever!

Palestrina's earnest desire was to prove the possibility of producing music which should be thoroughly devotional in character, and yet well adapted to the sacred words of the service. Finally, his eloquence and genius so prevailed that a committee was appointed to listen to three masses which he prepared, the first of which was to be sung in the Sistine Chapel on the 19th of June, 1565, as a test of his skill, and an example of what might be done if the rigorous laws deemed wise by many of the council were not put in force; but, on the contrary, the genius of the composer allowed sufficient liberty to work with melody, quartette, and choir, restricted, however, by certain rules which Palestrina himself was the readiest to suggest.

The great day came. We can fancy the excitement among all classes in Rome at the time, for the question was one of great importance. On the decision of the committee hung not only the fate of ecclesiastical music, but that of many people interested in the study of the art itself; and the poorest of the choir-boys as well as the most famous tenor singers appreciated how much this decision meant, while the large body of outsiders—the nobles, the ecclesiastics and dignitaries of Rome—the patrons of music, and the great throng of aspiring musicians and composers were full of an enthusiasm not less in quality because until the decision was fixed they were compelled to repress all expression of it.

Palestrina himself seems to have been so convinced that he was working in the right direction that he scarcely feared the result; and it shows how much the music which he wrote meant to him in its sacred form, when he plunged with such ardor into this occasion, since, of course, had he not met with approval in the church, many places in France and Germany would have been open to him for compositions of another character, and he would also have received much encouragement in Italy, even by his friends in the church, as a purely secular composer. But Palestrina's soul was with music of a different order: he longed to see sacred music elevated to its proper place; to see melody united with vocal art; to hear the words so sacred and so solemn to his devout ears wedded to the very best that belonged to his beloved art. It is said of Palestrina that on the night before the eventful day he remained alone in his study engaged in meditation and prayer, as a knight of olden time might watch the armor which for the first time he was to put on and go forth to the battle of life and the world, the triumph over flesh and the devil.

The mass which was ordered to be performed was afterwards known as the mass Papae Marcelli. The pope, the committee, and a host of the composer's friends, including all the famous people of Rome, assembled in the chapel; the music began; the solemn notes of the organ pealed forth, introducing to the enraptured hearers and to the world for all time to come music which may be considered as the most perfect of its kind, and from which later composers have had their keenest inspiration. A triumphant host of angels in the new Jerusalem, so said the pope himself, might have sung to the apostle of the apocalypse some such inspiring strains; and Cardinal Pisani, a famous musical critic, exclaimed in his delight, "So give from voice to voice in notes like these, and in the sweetness and piety of your hearts send forth strains which shall be forever inseparable from this occasion." The decision was fixed, and it was decided by the committee that this music of Palestrina's might be considered as embodying the style in which all future church-music should be composed. Perfect harmony was blended with solemnity and simplicity, and the heart and soul of the composer seemed to have been woven into the most artistic and finished portion of the work.

Palestrina was born of very humble parents in 1529, and as was usual with a boy who showed a talent for music at that time, he was sent to Rome, that his voice in a choir might attract attention and procure for him a musical education. The result was successful. From one point to another he progressed until the period of which I have told you, and from this point in his career up to the period of his death, in 1594, he composed ninety-three masses, besides hymns arranged for different festivals throughout the year, lamentations, litanies, magnificats, madrigals, and various similar pieces, all of which have been used from time to time in various Christian churches, and which may be heard on Christmas or Easter day throughout the whole country. To all of these he gave that exquisite character of piety and purity which were characteristic of his life; and as he was strongly in sympathy with St. Phillipo Neri, he embodied much of the loftiness of that saint's artistic spirit, and contrived, during his later years, to give to his religious works an even greater degree of solemnity, a breadth and strength which some of the earlier models lacked, although, at the same time, the melodic form was never wanting. It was in the arms of Phillipo Neri that he breathed his last on February 2, 1594.

Alessandro Scarlatti, Leo, and Durante followed Palestrina, and in 1733 Sebastian Bach wrote his famous mass in B minor. This was composed in true German spirit, and based upon what may be considered family principles, since we know that John Sebastian Bach was one of a long line of men of musical genius, who contributed from father to son a special kind of talent which characterizes all the work of the Bach family, and which in John Sebastian seemed to have reached that culminating point whence new sparks were struck in the old flame; but the fuel for the fire remained of the same material. This great mass of Bach's is more like an oratorio. It contains the most remarkable fugues, for which reason, more than any other, it is worth the careful consideration of the student; and in the opening of the *Credo* it shows one of the most perfect examples of the ancient *Canto Fermo* with modern harmonies, and with a masterly orchestral accompaniment.

The more recent Italian school of ecclesiastical music creates what is called and known among students as the ninth period. Durante gave it the first impulse; Pergo Lesi carried it on; Haydn and Mozart belonged to it exclusively; following them in the same line were Beethoven and Cherubini. Weber, Schubert, Hummel, Rossini, Mercedanti, and Gounod have written masses of a high order, but they have not kept strictly to the traditional forms for ecclesiastical music. Sentiment with them sometimes was allowed to interfere with solemnity, and the dramatic and emotional quality in their work is often more remarkable than its religious fervor.

In the Sistine Chapel, at the present day, mass music is

given in its perfection. On ordinary occasions thirty-two singers are employed: eight sopranos, eight altos, eight tenors, and eight bassos. On grand festivals the number is doubled, but very rarely is there any increase of orchestration or of instrumental accompaniment. The mass music is written with a plain signature, or with a single flat for the clef. Time is beaten in minims, except in the case of $\frac{3}{1}$, in which three semibreves are counted in each bar. After that part of the mass called the *Introit*, the choir takes up the *Kyrie Eleison*, the *Christi* next, and then the *Gloria*, which is generally a very triumphant portion of the mass, although certain portions of the mass are always to be taken in what is called adagio time. The *Credo* follows this; then the *Offertory*, where either a voluntary on the organ or a special solo is inserted; next the *Sanctus*, which is invariably a largo; next comes the last movement in the mass music, which is the *Agnus Dei*. After this are merely the responses and the words of the mass, which are spoken by the priest or deacon.

It would be impossible to give you in this volume more than a general idea of the importance of ecclesiastical music in the fifteenth century, with its effects upon the music of our own time. As I have said to you, all churches are now making use of the compositions of these early Italian and German masters, and their work has a special significance for the student of to-day. No matter what words are used in any church for the music composed originally for the Roman mass, the methods and treatment of that music must remain characteristic, and to the student they are more interesting when taken in connection with an entire work. Mozart's Twelfth Mass, Haydn's famous mass in B, Beethoven's and Rossini's requiems, several of Weber's masses, besides those of earlier composers, all now furnish the music for different Christian church services, and it will be worth the student's time and attention to make certain distinctions between old traditional forms: where the plain chant or early melodic form is used, where an idea like a *Canto Fermo* is worked out, and where the general impulse of the composer is allowed complete sway. Connected with such a study are certain points in harmony. For example, take the suggestions offered by that original *Kyrie* of which we have spoken, and then the fugues in Bach's mass in B minor. Study something about a fugue, and then examine one portion even of one of these, and gather therefrom as much material as possible for the next opportunity you have for listening to treatment of the same by the organist in your own church.

CHAPTER XII.

Ludwig von Beethoven.—Boyhood and First Studies.—At the Princess Lichnowsky's.—Cold Water and Compositions.—An Amusing Anecdote.—Sad Years.—"Adelaide."—Blind!—Last Days.

THERE is something about a great genius such as Beethoven's which makes one feel awestruck with a silent sort of homage to which words cannot pay sufficient tribute. Sculpture seems to do most, for in the cold, still grandeur of marble we can embody our ideas of homage of a master like the one whose story I wish to tell you here. The details of his sad and anxious and fretted life seem to fall away, to sink into insignificance; his petty failings, the burdens which tried and harassed him do not seem so much part of himself as the work which he has left us, which is immortal, even though he died without realizing its greatness, or its power for influencing the whole musical world. Beethoven's life began and ended with absolutely no personal satisfactions, for even his work was a sad sort of resource: his heart when heavily burdened found refuge in it. His work was the result of an instinct, but deafness and blindness overtook him in the midst of giving the world the noblest utterances of his poetic and inspired soul.

Ludwig von Beethoven was born at Bonn, December 16, 1770. His family had belonged originally to Louvain. His father and his grandfather were musicians in the court band of the Elector of Cologne; his father, being a tenor singer, was appointed to an official position in 1756. Jean Beethoven, the father of our musician, married the daughter of the chief cook at Ehrenbreitstein, a widow, who died when her son was seventeen, and who seems to have been beloved passionately by the boy. Both parents, although not very well off in this world's goods, loved music heartily, and seeing signs of a precocious talent very early in Ludwig, gave him every advantage; but the lad hated to practise, and to force him to the piano the father used to beat him unmercifully. However, with genius like his the drudgery of learning was soon over, and the child began to feel an influence towards composition. Various little things are preserved which he wrote between his seventh and ninth years, his earliest publication being the three sonatas for the pianoforte, published when he was eleven years of age, in 1781. One Pleiffer, a tenor singer, who joined the opera troupe in Bonn, and came to board with the Beethoven family, taught him for about a year, and meanwhile he learned the organ from a court organist who was enthusiastic over the child, then scarcely ten years of age; and he wrote a funeral cantata which was performed by the organist, and excited considerable discussion in the town.

When he was about eleven years of age, Ludwig accompanied his mother to Holland, travelling about and performing at various private houses where his precocious talent roused positive enthusiasm, although among the people whom he visited there was too little technical knowledge to make his genius really appreciated. However, it paved the way for the boy's success a little later, and at all events gave him a certain amount of confidence, and enabled him to try his hand at improvising, and above all things to criticise his own work.

It was about this time, when Beethoven was not twelve years of age, that the new organist at Bonn appointed him as his deputy during his absence in Munster, which shows what his ability must have been, since the music of the chapel was of a complicated description, and required skill both in the execution and the understanding necessary for its interpretation. However, the boy did so well that Neefe, the organist, declared he would become a second Mozart.

Soon after this we find Beethoven visiting "Papa Haydn," and presenting him with a cantata which he had composed. Haydn encouraged the lad greatly, and gave him some lessons, but Beethoven's inclination was more for Mozart's style than that of Haydn.

As soon as it was possible Beethoven established himself in Vienna, where Mozart's sudden death after a brilliant musical life had roused the Viennese people to a great necessity in the art. So Beethoven went to work and to study, and quickly gathered about him a circle of friends, among whom were some valuable and appreciative patrons.

At the house of Prince Lichnowsky he was always welcomed, the host and hostess doing everything to make him comfortable and happy, humoring his queer temper, his rough sort of teasing, and the peculiarities of his dress. Beethoven was always a clumsy, awkward figure in a drawing-room. He had a big head, with a shock of dark hair, and features only redeemed from absolute plainness by the soul that lay in the depths of his dark eyes and the smile that showed his brilliant white teeth. He cared nothing for his appearance, although he was so fond of washing, that one of his friends recorded that when really intent on any composition, it was his habit to fill a huge basin with water, and from time to time wash his hands and arms violently; meanwhile he would hum over his composition and return to his work with new ardor.

At the Lichnowskys he was humored in every way possible, the princess trying to make him feel free of all obligation; but it must sometimes have been hard to manage him. For instance, to make him feel that he was of first importance, the princess instructed her servants *always* to answer Beethoven's bell when it rang, without waiting even to attend to her orders.

The master, hearing of this, resented it deeply, and poor as he was insisted on having a servant of his own. Another story of his peculiar sensitiveness is of the time when they were rehearsing "Leonora," one of his grandest compositions. It so happened that the third bassoon was absent, and Beethoven, who was waiting to conduct the orchestra, lost all patience. Prince Lobkowitz, who was present, tried to make a joke of it, and to put him in good-humor.

"What harm done?" he said; "the first and second bassoon are here, don't mind a third!" Beethoven nearly danced with rage; and when the rehearsal was over he started for home, deliberately crossing the Platgoe Square to the gates of the Lobkowitz Palace, where he stood still and shouted up the entrance, "Donkey of a Lobkowitz! Donkey of a Lobkowitz!"

That his friends loved and humored him in spite of many such scenes, shows us how gentle and true a heart must really have beaten under his rough exterior.

He never married, although some of his music, sonatas

and songs, especially "Adelaide," were dedicated to the woman he asked vainly to be his wife, Countess Guiccardi; and needing some human being to care for and to make happy, he adopted his nephew Carl. I think no story could be sadder than that of Beethoven's love for this wretched boy, who abused his confidence in every way, and, indeed, by his wicked deceits broke the master's heart. Beethoven's letters are pathetic enough, but here and there some words sound like cries from his very soul. He begs Carl to come and see him—just to give him an hour—he is *so* lonely, and he has toiled and labored that the boy might know ease and comfort; but Carl was selfish, vain, and deceitful. Unless it were for money, he had no idea of spending any time with the uncle whose ill-health and disappointments were fast making him a fretful, melancholy invalid. Carl finally, after doing everything disreputable, enlisted, and Beethoven was forced to hear and know the extent of his deceit and villany; yet before he died, the old love and tenderness for his adopted child stirred in him, fanning the spark that had never quite been extinguished, and he added a codicil to his will—"I appoint my nephew Carl my sole heir."

Friendships and his glorious work might have done much for the master, but that his terrible misfortune of deafness came so soon upon him.

It was one day in 1800 that he asked his dear friend Ries

to walk out into the woods with him. There he acknowledged to Ries how fast he was growing deaf, and from that hour he seems to have felt that earthly joy was at an end. He could still lead his own works, but when the performance was ended he would have to be turned gently around to *see* the applause he could not hear! No wonder his friends tried to humor his passing waywardness when he was stricken with such a grief. He had loved to play and to compose at dark, and by holding his violin very near his face, for some time he contrived to *feel* the sweet sounds; but gradually these faded out of all hearing. At last we have a picture of him standing among his orchestra, deaf to all, and gradually growing blind!

The spectacle, the very thought of it is so sad that we turn to his lonely death-bed almost with relief. He loved to walk, and even when ill spent much time roaming about the country. "I wander about here with music-paper," he wrote, "among the hills and dales and valleys, and scribble a great deal. No man on earth can love the country as I do."

Happily this sympathy with nature remained always to cheer him, for, as his eyesight failed, he still *remembered* the visions of green and blossom which he had seen.

Although some money was found in his desk after death, he seems, during his life, to have had a terrible struggle with poverty, and would have died in actual want but for certain help from England. Not one loving word from the nephew Carl came to cheer his last hours, and on March 26, 1827, he passed away, glad of a release from life which meant now only pain and melancholy to the greatest master of his art the world has ever known. His tomb in Vienna bears emblems of life and death, with the one word *Beethoven*.

To attempt a criticism of Beethoven's work would be impossible. I often recall what I once heard a famous musician say when some younger man was questioning the master's work:

"We don't want anything better than what Beethoven gave us, *and no one ever got to the end of him yet.*"

How often the student may remember that! The variety is infinite; not one sonata, not one symphony but might contain study for a lifetime. Beethoven did not write impulsively. It is said that he went over and over his work; and, as you will find, it is always full of marks of expression so carefully made that you can be safe to follow every one, sure that it will produce precisely the desired effect.

A great deal of discussion has gone on of late years as to the time, or "tempo," as musical people say, in which the sonata should be played, and of late it seems to me that pianists are inclining to make the tempo much more rapid;

but no young student should attempt this, whatever they may hear in a concert-room. Take it all gradually, for *study* more than performance, and master each part, knowing as much of its meaning as you possibly can. No one can teach you more than you can learn in one sonata of Beethoven's. No orchestral performance can do more for you than one symphony of his, but critically examine *his* part. Take, for instance, the opening movements of the sonata popularly called the "Moonlight." In that alone lies the study of half a year, and yet how many young people dash at it, all unconscious of what a little *investigation* might do for them. Remember it is like a language, the words of which you must learn before you can express yourself. Every true artist *says* something of his own, which it is the part of the student to discover and then repeat in a voice to which he may give an expression of his own.

CHAPTER XIII.

Beethoven and the Concerto.—Explanation of this Form of Composition.
—Viadana.—Difference between Composers' Methods.—Cadenzas, and
what they mean.

ALTHOUGH the name of Beethoven must always be indelibly associated with the sonata, yet his modifications and improvements in that form of composition known as the *Concerto* make it seem to belong to the great master in a peculiar and permanent fashion. Mozart gave to the concerto its first idea of permanence, and it was founded upon the sonata. The name is intended to express an instrumental composition, which is expressly designed to display the skill of one performer on an instrument, and which is accompanied by an orchestra. The first notice we have of any concerto was one written in 1603 by a composer named Viadana, for voices and organ. Other instruments were added later, and in 1686 Torvelli published a concerto for two violins and a bass. The sonata, as you know, grew out of the suite, and the concerto was the result of the sonata, but of course a general idea characterizes them all. The concertos of different masters are, of course, as different as are their different styles, and yet a certain set of rules are observed in their composition. A concerto consists of three movements, while the scherzo, which is used in the sonata, is excluded. The first movement in Mozart's concertos begins with what is called a *tutti* passage for the orchestra. This tutti ends in the original key and not in the dominant or the relative major, as would have to be the case in a sonata if the composition were in a minor key. Following this comes the solo, whether of piano or other instrument. A repetition of the beginning follows as a general rule, in which the honors are divided between the solo instrument and the orchestra. The second subject is produced precisely as we have had in a sonata, and in this the first solo portion almost invariably is brought to a brilliant close in the key of the dominant or the relative major. For instance, supposing it to be written in the key of C, the solo in the second part would end in G. Then follows another tutti, a second solo, and, like the sonata, it is worked up and down, and finally back to the original key. Mr. Prout, in an admirable explanation of Mozart's concertos, mentions the fact that in many old concertos, near the end of the last tutti, upon the chord on the dominant, a pause is made for the introduction of a cadenza by the soloist. I have heard this done several times in modern concertos, notably in one or two of Beethoven's, especially prepared for the Sunday concerts in Paris, and I have no doubt such variations are constantly made. Beethoven wrote many such cadenzas for his own concertos. With him the custom was to conclude the cadenza with a long shake on the chord of the dominant seventh. The orchestra, then, in a short but fine passage concludes the movement. Sometimes it is the soloist who is passive during this pause, and the orchestra who round the movement. This is specially noteworthy to the young student, because the cadenza, being to a certain extent outside matter, may be subject to special criticism and analysis, and is useful since it must be characteristic both of the composer's genius and the skill of the player. Beethoven decided to give greater prominence to the orchestra in his concertos. Mozart had made the orchestra subservient to the soloist. Also Beethoven connected the second and third movements in his concertos, examples of which are to be found in the concertos in G and E flat. Mendelssohn followed this precedent so closely that in the piano-forte concertos of G minor and D minor the movements are continuous. In Beethoven's concerto in G, and the one in E flat, he entirely broke away from the long established custom of opening a concerto with a tutti for the orchestra. The concerto in G opens with the piano alone; in E flat the piano enters on the second bar. Mozart had only once, and then in a concerto rarely played, tried this experiment.

We must call the student's attention to one more modification of Beethoven's. In the concerto in E flat, Opus 73, Beethoven writes (instead of leaving the pause for the cadenza) one of his own, adding the note, "Don't make a cadenza, but go on at once to the following"—the cadenza being, from the nineteenth bar, closely followed by the orchestra. All of these facts are interesting, and a strict attention to them, when hearing or reading any of the concertos referred to, cannot fail to impress upon the student's mind the motive and the method of the works themselves; and they have their strong significance in the history of various compositions, helping us to a more intelligent understanding of what we hear or study. Mendelssohn did not insert in his piano-forte concertos any cadenza at all, nor has Brahms. Schumann and Raff have made some variations in the form of the concerto—Schumann being one of the composers of modern times who has taken liberties with facility and grace; and Liszt's concertos for piano and orchestra are composed upon a plan so different from any one else, that they can scarcely be regarded in the light of anything but fantasias. The concerto is regarded by celebrated pianists as the most sympathetic method of displaying their own powers; hence this style of composition should be closely studied by all students of the piano-forte.

CHAPTER XIV.

Carl Maria von Weber.—Story of his Life.—A Baby Prodigy.—Anecdote of his Life at the Court of Wurtemberg.—"Der Freischütz."—In London with Moscheles.—A Last Visit.—Asleep.—Overtures and their Origin.—Structure.—Weber's Work.—Mendelssohn's Use of the Term.—Overtures of English Composers.

During the year 1784 a German nobleman named Von Weber arrived in Vienna with his little children, whose musical abilities were so marked that the father determined to give them every advantage within his power. But Baron von Weber was poor and reckless. He had always been a spendthrift, and was noted for his eccentric habits and ideas. Being the uncle of Mozart, he imagined that in Vienna he might force his children into a place as prominent as that filled by the famous young composer. But this was not to be the case. His sons were placed under the care of "Papa Haydn," but did not distinguish themselves; and meanwhile the penniless, good-looking father, a widower of fifty, fell in love with the very young daughter of his landlord, a beautiful girl of sixteen, who seems to have consented readily to marry him.

The newly wedded pair went almost at once to the town of Eutin, where the Herr Baron was offered the place of *Stadtmusikant*, or town musician. This was rather a downward step, but it at least gave his little wife food and shelter. Old Weber seemed to have no idea that she needed more in her life than its actual necessaries. He treated her harshly, if not with absolute cruelty, and in 1798, when her one child, Carl Maria von Weber, was eleven years of age, the poor little mother faded out of life.

Carl was born at Eutin in 1786. He was always delicate, sensitive, and over-studious, and from his birth his rough-tempered father determined to make a musical prodigy of him. What hours of suffering he must have endured as a mere baby, forced to sit at the piano, his little fingers strained upon the keys, while his father, with a baton that could any moment become a rod, stood over him!

As a mere child Weber began to compose, and his father carried him about from place to place, sometimes staying long enough to have one master really influence the boy, but rarely giving him time to think out carefully the music that he was urged on to compose. Much of his time was passed behind the scenes of provincial theatres; and although the influence of this sort of life on his moral character could not have been good, it helped him when he came to write for the stage. He learned by constant ob-

CARL MARIA VON WEBER.

servation everything connected with the workings of the opera.

After a youth spent in many wanderings, and with hardships and disappointments of various kinds, young Weber, at twenty-one, was appointed private secretary to the brother of the King of Wurtemberg, and in this position he might have been successful but for a curious quarrel with the king.

This monarch was a man of low tastes, coarse manners, and extremely bad temper. Poor Weber was often his victim, for in his character of the duke's secretary he had to beg from the king whenever his Majesty's very reckless brother needed money or any other royal favor. On such occasions the king vented all his wrath on Weber, and treated him at times with insult and contempt. One day, after an unusually wild scene with the king, Weber left the royal apartments, feeling as if he could no longer endure such an existence. He stumbled against an untidy-looking old woman, who inquired where she could find the royal washer-woman.

Weber was still boiling over with rage he had been compelled to conceal in the king's presence, and on a mad impulse he pointed to the door of the king's cabinet, saying, "There!" In walked the unsuspicious old woman, who, without recognizing the king, informed his Majesty that the young gentleman outside had told her she would find the washer-woman there. The king, who was well-known to hate old women, sprang up, poured forth a volley upon the terrified intruder, and ordered Weber to be thrown into prison at once. Later he was released; but the incident was never forgotten by the king, who, when an opportunity came, revenged himself.

Weber's father had become involved in business difficulties, and Carl generously tried to shield the old man from disgrace. But while Carl's opera of St. Sylvana was in rehearsal, and likely to make a great success, the king had both father and son arrested. A mock trial was arranged, and the king himself presided over it with his usual fury of temper and expression. Young Weber remained calm and dignified, even when he listened to the sentence of banishment pronounced upon his father and himself, and left Wurtemberg completely resolved to devote all his heart and mind to the pursuit of music.

A new era in his life followed. He wrote with clearer mind and greater success, and as soon as he freed himself from certain evil influences of his life, the very best part of his nature developed. It is comforting to think how happy Weber was in his marriage. His wife was a young artist, of exquisite temperament and disposition, whom he loved devotedly, and who made his home-life as perfect as it could be, when we remember how many cares he had, and that for years he suffered with a fatal disease. It was for his wife, his dear Lina, that he composed the "Invitation to the Waltz," ever since so famous as a piano-forte piece, and it was under much of her inspiration that he wrote the opera of "Der Freischütz."

This great work was performed for the first time in Berlin, in 1821, and Weber and his wife spent some time in that city preparing for its production. In those days, even more than at present, musicians suffered greatly from the effects of their rivals to lower them and their work in public estimation, and Weber was not spared such annoyances. But he felt an enthusiasm in his art which entirely mastered this petty side of life; and Sir Julius Benedict, then his pupil, tells us how Weber spent the day preceding the production of the opera. He passed some time at the piano, going over a new work upon which he was engaged, and gave Sir Julius and Lina the ideal story he had in it. The music was the since famous concert piece in F minor, and it seemed that never had the master played better or been in a calmer and loftier mood. He then took a light dinner and had a little rest, and so, with his wife and favorite pupil, went to the opera-house. A great audience was assembled, and among them a little bright-eyed boy, who sat entranced, an eager listener at his father's side.

The boy was destined later to be famous as Felix Mendelssohn-Bartholdy. The success was complete. The composer was received like a hero of victory, and slight and awkward as he was, he stood among his friends great for that hour at least. The royalty of genius was about him, and every one paid homage to it.

Unhappily Weber was not always destined to such triumphs. Five years passed away, and we find him in London, where he was already famous as the composer of several operas—"Der Freischütz," "Euryanthe," "Oberon." But though the latter proved a great success, the public did not receive Weber as his friends felt that he deserved to be received. Moscheles, the composer and musician, the loyal, earnest friend of art and its disciples, with Sir George Smart and several others, did all that they could to make Weber a successful, happy visitor in the English capital; but Weber was fast dying, and every trouble in his public life seemed to reduce his failing strength.

A dear old friend has told me of her last visit from Weber—how he toiled up-stairs to her bright drawing-room, and, sinking into a chair, declared himself too ill to have ventured out. But even at the very last he continued patient and gentle. On the evening of the 4th of June, 1826, his friends saw him for the last time. As usual, he retired alone and bolted his door. In the morning the servant who went to call him got no response. He hastened to Sir George Smart, who with Moscheles burst into his room. They found him lying dead, as in a peaceful sleep, his head resting on his arm, his expression one of pure and gentle repose.*

The meaning of the word *overture* is literally *opening*, and in its original use had reference to the prelude to an opera; but after the close of the seventeenth century it began to take form more as a special kind of composition, and later came to be considered as of direct musical importance. In the time of the composer Lulli, the *overture* was only a sort of introduction in very slow time, occasionally followed by an allegro, with certain repetition and suggestions of the music which was to follow it. Handel gave the overture a prominent place and character. Gluck strove to identify the music of his overtures with what was to follow in the opera, and at the same time to preserve its own characteristics.

The overture has shown in many instances the same principles of structure which belong to the first or second movements of a symphony or a sonata, and Rossini, who has

---

* A dear friend of Weber told me that it was quite untrue that the so-called "Weber's last Waltz" was found under his pillow. It was not even written by him, but by one of his pupils.

composed admirable overtures, made a special point of what is called the *crescendo*. (Note in his work also the use of the *dominant* of the key before the tonic.) Beethoven is considered to have outrivalled all his predecessors in No. 3 of the four overtures which he wrote for his grand opera of "Fidelio." The theme of the opera is exquisitely portrayed in this overture, and for dramatic effect can scarcely be excelled. Weber's overtures to his operas take so distinct a place in the history of music that his name must be forever associated with this form of composition where it is used as a prelude. In the overture to "Der Freischütz" he makes use of the orchestra in the most skilful and ingenious manner, suggesting all the characteristics of the opera in the most masterly style; and unless we consider Wagner's overture to "Lohengrin" or the "Tannhauser," no modern composer has rivalled him.

The name as well as the form of overture now refers also to a special orchestral piece intended for performance in public, whereby the composer can illustrate some special allegorical or poetical subject. Mendelssohn's overtures known as the "Hebrides," "A Calm Sea and a Prosperous Voyage," are famous examples of this kind, and the Shakespearian prelude which he composed as a boy, and which he later combined with more dramatic music for "Midsummer Night's Dream," is regarded as a surprising work of art

RICHARD WAGNER.

and sentiment. Berlioz, Schumann, Sterndale-Bennett, Sir Julius Benedict, and many other composers of modern times, have given special attention to overtures of this kind, and in studying the subject try to investigate also those forms of composition known as *Introductions* and *Preludes*, and remember that the *Overture* and *Symphony* have much in common.

CHAPTER XV.

The Orchestra of Yesterday and To-day.—Its Origin.—Distinction between Orchestras and Bands.—A Wedding Celebration in the Sixteenth Century.—The Duc de Joyeuse.—Lutes and Viols.—The First Orchestra on Record.—Italian Developments.—Scarlatti's Obligato.—One Hundred Years of Progress.—List of Instruments.—Chamber Music.—A Conductor's Responsibility.—The First Use of the Baton.—Mendelssohn's Facility in remembering Work.—An old Sketch-book.

THROUGHOUT the story of music and musicians, so far as we have been able to follow it, you will remember certain indications or suggestions here and there of what may be considered the beginning of the orchestra, and in this chapter I wish to tell you something more definite concerning it, before reaching the life of a famous leader or conductor—Felix Mendelssohn-Bartholdy.

When you attend a concert and see before you the orderly and systematically arranged rows of musicians; when you listen to their rendering of some fine work, such as Beethoven's Fourth, Fifth, or Ninth Symphony, some overture of Weber's, some concerto of Mendelssohn's or symphony of Bach's, it will be interesting to you to have learned whence came the knowledge, or I may say the science, of this arrangement. The story of the orchestra will tell you this.

The word is taken from the Greek. It really means an open space where people sit, but in the present acceptation of the term it expresses a place for an instrumental band and a chorus; and properly speaking, an orchestra *must* sit.

This is one of the chief distinctions between an *orchestra* and a *band*. Bands, by right, stand while they play, orchestras ought to sit—that is, unless the weight of their instruments compels them to stand. Besides this distinction, a band is composed of wind instruments; an orchestra has both wind and stringed instruments.

The first orchestra of which we have any record sufficiently correct to make us certain that such a term could be applied to it, was in the sixteenth century.

In France there lived a certain famous nobleman, the Duc de Joyeuse. The splendor and beauty of his entertainments were renowned, and he was noted for his interest in everything which appertained to the art of music. Wandering minstrels always found a hospitable shelter within his gates. Even the most ordinary dancers of the time were welcomed, provided they could accompany themselves upon any musical instrument, and "dance therewith tunefully and harmoniously." At that time lutes, viols, and flutes of various kinds were used with cornets, drums, and trumpets, and some instruments which had been brought to Europe by returning Crusaders. These were combined together in a sort of rude fashion, but with no reference to harmony or their relation to each other; for which reason, as you may well imagine, performances upon them, however numerous or skilled the players, could scarcely be considered *orchestral*. However, the Duc de Joyeuse believed that something better might be done. On the occasion of his marriage with the Lady Margaret of Lorraine, he and some of his musical friends determined upon producing something decidedly novel in the way of musical entertainment out of the abundance of crude material before them. An orchestra with a certain degree of harmony in arrangement was the result. This was in 1581. Old accounts still exist of this performance given at the Château de Moutiers. It was called the "Ballet comique de la Royne," and although as an orchestral performance it had in it the same elements which make it appear to us almost absurd, at the same time there was the foundation laid for the genuine orchestra. We read that "ballet-dancers in full dress" performed upon the violins, while others played upon flutes and some upon harps, the entire spectacle being a very gorgeous and brilliant one, and the music considered by the spectators as something novel and delightful.

From this point we can follow the story of the orchestra

rapidly. In Italy the impulse towards music was so widespread that the orchestra was speedily developed. In 1600 we read of one as attached to an oratorio, and a quaint suggestion is offered by the composer of the oratorio. He desires that the characters in the drama should be asked to carry instruments in their hands, and play, or *seem* to play, during the symphonies!

When music became very dramatic in form, when oratorio and opera developed an interest in special accompanists, the orchestra naturally grew in strength and proportion, and asserted itself as a distinct form of musical performance. Scarlatti wrote fine music for two violins—a viola and bass —making use of them exactly as all composers in every school of music have ever since. According to Dr. Burney, a well-known authority at the end of the last century, Scarlatti wrote an obligato especially for one instrument in the orchestra.

Within a hundred years from that performance at the Château de Montiers the orchestra had reached a point when we can find in it all the elements now in use. The stringed band was the foundation then as now, and wind instruments were used to "enlarge or to beautify the structure of the rest by its efforts, and separated by its firm tone and massive proportions." Bach entered thoroughly into the spirit of the orchestra, and arranged his work for it with the greatest possible regard for delicacy and expression. He objected to making his "effects" too powerful, having a distaste for the thunderous in sound or the overwhelming, and accordingly much of his orchestral music is so arranged that many critics even of the present day consider it thin and ineffective. But his purpose was not so much to display the power and figure of an orchestra as to make the instruments carry out the idea of spirit and finish in the composer's work, and at the same time to support it by a volume of sound without doing anything to produce too great a strain upon the hearer's capacity. Handel, Mozart, and Beethoven worked at the orchestra indefatigably, realizing its capabilities and appreciating that a great field lay before them; that, of necessity, much more could be done than had ever been attempted with a finely organized and conducted orchestra.

The most accomplished pianist can learn a constant lesson from hearing a good orchestra perform the well-known works of great masters; and in listening to any such performance try to observe carefully the different instruments, how they are used, to what purpose the composer has put them, and precisely how far each one influences the whole. A most interesting and useful study is to find out before hearing any orchestral performance the names of the various instruments used, and by means of a dictionary or encyclopædia to learn all that is possible about them, the result of which will be that your understanding and your entertainment will be decidedly enlarged, and no doubt a concert seem thereby to be transformed to you.

Here is a list of the instruments of a complete orchestra: first violins, 15; second violins, 12; violas, 10; violoncellos, 10; double basses, 8; flutes, 2; piccolo, 1; oboes, cor Anglais, clarionet, corno di bassetto, bassoon, double bassoon, trumpets, horns, trombones, timpani, cornet-à-piston, bass trumpet, tenor tuba, ophicleide, contra bass tuba, harp, bass drum, cymbals. The number and kind of instruments can of course be varied to a certain extent without losing the effect.

Chamber music differs from ordinary orchestras because none of the instruments are doubled—that is, only one of a kind is included in it, and it is adapted to a small number of performers on stringed instruments.

Until the beginning of this century the conductor of an orchestra sat at a harpsichord among the instruments, and his regulation of the orchestra seems to have consisted only in keeping a watchful eye upon them and now and then striking a few chords when there was danger of their going wrong. Even as late as 1829 Mendelssohn conducted in this fashion his symphony in C minor at the Philharmonic Concert in London; but very speedily the baton took its place, and about the same time the position of the so-called "leader" of the orchestra became obsolete. The leader's duty had been to keep the band together, but, as he stood among the violins, he had very slight control upon the larger number of the orchestra. In the autobiography of Spohr the musician, he gives us a picture of the early condition of things, and also of a concert at which he was to direct, when he insisted upon leading with a baton and directing from the front. "Henceforth," to quote the autobiography, "no one was ever again seen seated at the piano during the performance of symphonies and overtures." A series of concerts given in 1845 in London were conducted by Sir Henry Bishop and Moscheles, the conductor working indefatigably then, as at all times, for the advancement of what was best in musical art, never desiring to promote his own personal interests or even popularity at the risk of anything which should retard the progress of science and culture in music. Believing firmly that the true way to conduct an orchestra was in the present approved fashion, he strove to forward it, and at length, in 1846, Signor, now Sir Michael, Costa announced a concert, and his name simply as "conductor" appeared upon the programme for the first time. The part of the conductor cannot be too highly valued. Upon his enthusiasm, as well as his knowledge of the work being performed, depends largely the success of any performance; and the finest feeling must be combined with the very finest qualities of a true musician, and at the same time conductor and performers must be entirely in harmony and have worked their way through many rehearsals, so that a familiarity exists, without which their final performance cannot be a sympathetic one. Among the many conductors of the past century and a half Handel and Mendelssohn rank supreme, but the latter united all the qualities of a true-born conductor with those of a thorough musician. Beethoven could not conduct, not only because of his deafness, but because of his curious disposition. Schumann, who had certain elements of a fine conductor about him, was too absent-minded for the work. Moscheles would have been one of the first conductors of the age had he had time to devote to the work; and Mendelssohn stands in this century entirely alone. The conductor must study the score, must correct all the parts, often rearrange them, see that they are perfectly marked, and take the responsibility of the interpretation given the work which his orchestra performs.

Very many stories are told by Mendelssohn's friends of how, on certain occasions, when parts of the score were found missing, just as the men were taking their places, the sympathetic conductor always contrived in some fashion to get the work together again: his marvellous faculty for rapid musical work often coming to the rescue of himself and his band. Once, on a very important occasion, while the audience were waiting, he dashed off a whole part, writing it from memory.

In an old house in London there was, not long ago, a book full of Mendelssohn's sketches, when he and Moscheles were on their concert tour; and looking at them—some bright, some humorous, all happy and kindly—one can fancy just how much heart and soul Mendelssohn put into his work. He put his fun into it as well as his pathos. Indeed, whatever the great musician had, he gave it all to those around him when he stood in the conductor's place.

CHAPTER XVI.

Felix Mendelssohn-Bartholdy.—Work and Play.—The Juvenile Orchestra. —A Pretty Picture.—Fanny Mendelssohn.—A Famous Journey.—A Letter from Goethe's House.—Moscheles in Berlin.—A Memorable Evening.—The E-flat Concerto.—Work and Recreation.—Fanny's Marriage.—In London and at Birmingham.—With the Moscheleses.— A Happy Marriage.—Founding the Conservatory of Leipsic.—Fanny's Sudden Death.—The "Elijah."—"And behold, the Lord passed by." —Last Days.

ABOUT the year 1820, a musician in Berlin name Ferdinand Hiller used to watch with interest the games played by certain clever little fellows led by a particularly handsome lad of ten years. This boy, whose name was Felix Mendelssohn-Bartholdy, was quaintly dressed, and had the air of distinction which was natural to the Mendelssohn family. He entered into every game with such spirit and delight that Hiller was amazed to learn that he was a musical genius whose composition and performances were all known to an intimate circle of friends.

Mendelssohn's father was a banker living in the Leipzigerstrasse, Berlin, and Felix, his eldest son, was born in 1809. He had one brother and two sisters, and never was a family circle more thoroughly happy and harmonious. Music was highly esteemed in the household, but, at the same time, it was a disappointment when Felix decided upon a musical career. However, the parents were wise enough to see that their son possessed real genius, and so they set to work to give him the best possible education. So keen was his eye and ear for harmony that when he was only seven years old, and took lessons of old Zelter, he called the master's attention to a curious error in a piece of Sebastian Bach's. This was the recurrence of six consecutive fifths, and it was this remarkable keenness of ear which made him later so remarkable as the conductor of a great orchestra.

Felix composed, as I have said, while he was still romping with little playfellows in the Berlin streets, and once a week his father allowed him to assemble certain young musicians and lead them through some orchestral work. One of his most enthusiastic friends has given us a charming picture of these "practices"—the group of earnest performers, the boy conductor, still wearing his childish costume the round jacket and deep collar, standing on a raised platform, baton in hand, solemnly and most correctly directing the players.

Felix's sister Fanny was his special favorite and companion. She was a brilliant musician and composed readily,

FELIX MENDELSSOHN-BARTHOLDY.

Mendelssohn's Visit to Goethe.

although with less genius, perhaps, than Felix. Several of the "Songs without Words" were written by her. Never was there the slightest jealousy or any misunderstanding between the two; their work and their recreation went together in complete harmony. When Felix composed anything, he could scarcely wait to show it to his dear "Fance," as he would call her. Everything which the two young people liked they shared with each other, and yet the two little ones, Paul and Rebecca, were not shut out. It was a charming quartet, and no wonder that the friends of the Mendelssohns used to fear the young people would be spoiled by knowing only the happy, prosperous side of life.

In 1821 Felix made a famous journey. Zelter, his old master, was a dear friend of the poet Goethe, and through him came an invitation to the little boy to pass a fortnight in the house of the great man. It was certainly a memorable visit, and Felix, although only eleven years of age, wrote charming letters to his parents and his sister, describing his experiences. From the first of these I quote:

"He [Goethe] does not look like a man of seventy-three; rather of fifty. After dinner Fraulein Ulrike, Frau von Goethe's sister, asked him for a kiss, and I followed her example. Every morning I have a kiss from the author of 'Faust' and 'Werther,' and every afternoon two kisses from father and friend Goethe. Think of that! In the afternoon I played to Goethe for about two hours, partly fugues of Bach, and partly improvisations. In the evening they arranged a whist-table, and Professor Zelter, who took a hand, said, 'Whist means that you are to hold your tongue.'"

The attention that he received during this visit does not seem to have touched Felix's sweet nature with anything like affectation or vanity. He returned home ready to enter into family affairs, studies, recreation, and the like, and to give them all accounts of his sojourn in Weimar, and apparently forgetting most of the compliments which had been paid him there.

In 1824 concerts of fine instrumental music were rare even in Berlin, and so the advent of Ignaz Moscheles, a famous virtuoso and composer, was hailed with delight, and the excitement which attended the purchase of tickets for his first concert was something surprising. Moscheles was to play Bach, Beethoven, and Mozart, and also a concerto of his own—the since famous one in E-flat major, and which is a tremendous work for any pianist even at the present day. While he was performing this concerto, Moscheles observed among his listeners a slight, handsome lad with flushed face, and dark eyes brilliant with excitement. Now and then the boy would glance across at a tall gentleman not far away, who always responded to his look with a pleasant smile and nod of his head. Moscheles looked also at the tall gentleman, and as soon as he had finished playing he approached him and inquired cordially,

"Now, friend Kapellmeister, are you satisfied?"

The Herr Kapellmeister thus addressed was the famous musician Hummel, and he replied in terms of great enthusiasm, and added:

"My young friend, Felix Mendelssohn, is waiting to speak to you." The boy pressed eagerly forward and caught Moscheles by the hand. Something was said about the music, and then Moscheles accompanied Hummel and the Mendelssohns back to the house of the latter, where a supper was given, the children being permitted to remain up; and the meal being at an end, the entire party adjourned to the music-room, where until daylight one after another of the famous musicians present performed to the never-wearying delight of their listeners, Moscheles astonishing every one by his marvellous extempore playing, old Zelter suddenly turning around and exclaiming, "Come, Felix, let us see whether you can show any credit to your teachers. Sit down and play whatever comes into your head."

It seems to me that the scene which followed evidences more completely than anything which had occurred in his previous life the true genius of Felix Mendelssohn. Instead of rushing to the piano and giving a display of his skill, the boy shrank back, turning pale and declaring that he could not play a note.

Zelter was enraged, and declared that he would write to Goethe that the boy Felix had turned coward.

"After playing at grand concerts at Weimar," exclaimed Zelter, "is this the way you are going to show the white feather?"

"But," exclaimed Felix, "at that time I did not rightly know what I was doing; and now, after those two there"— indicating Moscheles and Hummel — "I neither can nor ought to play." And with this he rushed from the room, bursting into tears.

By request Moscheles left the E-flat major concerto, and the next day, to his great astonishment, Felix performed it for him in such a superb manner that Moscheles declared it would be impossible for him to consider himself in the light of the lad's teacher.

Soon after this we find Mendelssohn composing various works—operas, symphonies, etc., and especially the music of the "Midsummer Night's Dream;" soon after which he began to dream of his greatest work, the oratorio "Elijah."

Fanny Mendelssohn's marriage did not remove her from the charmed family circle. Just back of her father's house was a beautiful villa known as the Garden House, and here she and her husband, the artist Hensel, took up their abode. Here she organized the celebrated matinees of music, at which the flower of Berlin musical and aristocratic society was present, and where the noblest compositions were performed week after week.

Felix's English journeys which he made from time to time were full of pleasures, both musical and social. With his dear friends the Moscheleses he stayed constantly, and in the house many pictures and other reminders of those happy, busy days when Felix and Moscheles worked together still remain. Moscheles had a fund of delightful humor, and he and Felix seemed just fitted to draw out that which was most entertaining in each other.

Sometimes, after hard work, Mendelssohn would come into Madame Moscheles's drawing-room, tired and worn. Then that ever-ready friend knew just what should be done. She would insist upon his lying down in a darkened room, where he would often sleep for hours. These long sleeps were his salvation, for there was in his family a disposition to sudden brain prostration.

It was Mendelssohn's habit to compose rapidly, and then to correct and recorrect some of his best phrases, until sometimes Moscheles would have to insist upon his friend's leaving his MSS. further untouched. But Mendelssohn was never satisfied: he would yield grumblingly, and declare he never could write *just* what he wanted. But to what genius is any work perfect?

Mendelssohn's wife Cecile was beautiful, amiable, and sympathetic, and she proved a devoted companion to him and a most careful mother. When Mendelssohn and Moscheles undertook the guidance of the Leipsic Conservatoire, Felix's house became a new social and artistic circle, and Hiller has given a graphic description of it.

There was a large dining-room, with a sitting-room and bedrooms opening from it. To the left was Felix's study, a water-color drawing of which now hangs in Madame Moscheles's London home. Here were his piano, desk, and some favorite pictures, and the small portable easel or writing-stand, now also in Madame Moscheles's possession, which he constructed himself, and on which he composed most of the "Elijah."

One evening a friend found Mendelssohn seated, buried in thought, before his Bible. He looked up with one of those sudden gleams which used to transfigure his whole face. "Listen," he said; and then, in a voice full of agitation, he read that part of the First Book of Kings beginning, "And, behold, the Lord passed by." It had inspired him for the "Elijah."

Those few short years in Leipsic must have afforded delightful memories for the friends who flocked to Felix's house. Not only was there constantly good music, but on birthdays and other festive occasions the Moscheleses and Mendelssohns would improvise most delightful entertainments, into which the great artists entered with childlike enthusiasm. On one of these occasions, in which Joachim, the celebrated violinist, took a part, Moscheles writes that " Mendelssohn was sitting on a large straw arm-chair, which creaked under his weight as he rocked to and fro, and the room echoed with his peals of laughter."

Felix was at Frankfort when news was brought him of his sister Fanny's sudden death. She had been playing at one of her matinees—her fingers suddenly dropped from the keys — she was carried into an anteroom, and soon breathed her last. From that time Felix's spirits drooped. Not only did he mourn his sister's loss, but her early death seemed to be prophetic of his own.

On the 9th of October, 1847, he composed his last work, "The Night Song." That same day he came to see the Moscheleses, walking slowly through their garden, and then going out with his friends for a stroll, during which he talked of Cecile and her coming birthday. From this he went to the home of an intimate friend, Frau Frege. There he attempted some music, but was forced to give it up. He went home, and a little while after his wife found him pale and cold upon the sofa. The next day the symptoms of brain trouble began, and on November 4, 1847, he expired, at the age of thirty-eight years.

It has been given to few human beings to pass a life so unclouded by care or sadness, so full of love and sympathy and the joys of success, as Felix Mendelssohn's. In the thirty-eight years of his life he included more work and more simple joy than many who live beyond the allotted threescore-years-and-ten, and it is a relief to turn from sad lives, such as Mozart's or Weber's or even Beethoven's, to one like his. Everything sweet, everything that was tinged with the sadness which comes over any artistic spirit, you can find in his "Songs without Words;" everything grand and sublime in his oratorios of "Elijah" and "St. Paul."

When he lay dead his earliest intimate friend, Edward Devrient, tells us that he seemed to be buried in flowers, for to his bier his friends brought everything that was rare and fragrant in that November season. He looked, Devrient said, once more as he had looked when a boy. Devrient, who had been his tenderest companion, kissed his brow for the last time, and of that moment he writes—
"The span of time in my remembrance enclosed the whole of happy youth in one perfect indelible thought."

IGNATZ MOSCHELES.

CHAPTER XVII.

A Trio : Chopin, Schubert, and Schumann.—Chopin in Paris.—Anecdote of a Memorable Visit.—Flowers and Nocturnes.—A Brief Story.—Schubert's Life.—Teaching School and Composing.—One Stormy Afternoon.—"The Erl King."—Beethoven's Friendship.—Last Days.—Robert Schumann.—A Brilliant Genius.—Little Clara Wieck.—A Happy Marriage.—Sad Years.—His Last Hours.

THREE composers seem to occur to our minds together—François Frederick Chopin, Franz Schubert, and Robert Schumann. For myself, the music of Chopin seems always to suggest certain scenes in his life, and some of it involuntarily brings to mind a scene described by an old friend.

It was in Paris, when Chopin was about twenty-five years of age, a slim, refined-looking young man with a gay smile, although very melancholy eyes, and my friend and her painter cousin met him in the market-place of the Madeleine buying violets and some other spring flowers, after which they all walked across the sunshiny square together to Chopin's apartment, where he had a charming salon full of softly tinted draperies, of flowers, some dusky old portraits, and some water-colors, light in tone and delicate in sentiment. Chopin was in excellent musical humor. He played for them, going from one thing to another until nearly evening. He improvised, and would turn his head back from the piano, looking from one to another, well knowing the sympathy he would read in their faces. My friend told me that her memories of Chopin at the piano, as on this occasion, were very wonderful and precious to her. Sometimes he would grow absorbed, and look like the embodiment of his own most melancholy music, but his touch was light and flexible; no one, unless it was Moscheles, Liszt, or Rubinstein, ever played his impromptus in any way as well as he did himself. No musician's work seemed so entirely part of the composer's very soul—to be the outcome of his own personal feelings, his own fancies, his wild, fantastic, and pathetic longings; and for this reason one likes to think of him at the piano in the beautiful room, playing, improvising, and, as it were, dreaming over the strange chords, the brilliant arpeggios and bewildering chromatic passages, while all about were the fragrances of spring flowers, violets and daffodils, a heaping jar of narcissus, and great bowls of lilacs, white and purple, mingling their odors with the dreamy sounds. I wished that my friend had had more to tell me of that one day in Paris. Somehow, as I have said, Chopin's music calls it readily to mind. He had gone out to buy the flowers as a sort of inspiration; and certainly the music that resulted always lived in my friend's memory—

part of her thought of the man himself, for Chopin's music was distinctly personal. Some critics think it overladen with sentimentality, an element young players are too apt to get into their style, and certainly to be strictly avoided; but Chopin, it seems to me, had too much real genius to make this predominate. Everything he wrote has its tinge of melancholy, everything has a little undercurrent of fanciful feeling, which breaks out now and then, like the spray of a fountain, into something which ends in thin air before you can catch all its lights; but the foundation is solid, and when you play any of Chopin's music, remember not to be carried away by the idea that it is all to be expressed in lightness and delicacy. Try to find the deeper thought first, and then weave your daintiest feeling of the music about it.

Chopin's history was brief, and melancholy at the last. He was born February 8, 1810, at Zelazowa-Wola, a Polish village near Warsaw, and he died at Paris in 1849. His father, who was French, settled in Warsaw, where he was a professor at the Academy, and where he had also a first-class private school. Little Frederic was brought up with lads of refinement and good-breeding, so that, as a child, he saw little of the roughness of life. His mother, who was a Polish lady of extremely sensitive temperament, gave him his first ideas of poetry and romance, and perhaps from her he inherited the tinge of melancholy which followed him through life. But as a youth he was gay enough, fond of amusements and all sorts of fun.

Before he was nineteen he had become a finished pianist, and as this was only in 1828, it was more of a feat than it could be now. His teachers and friends were anxious for him to be known and applauded in the world, and so he went from Poland to Vienna, where he quickly gathered a circle of friends about him, who listened and admired as much as his dearest masters could wish. At this time every one interested in any way in music, whether as an art or in performance, was full of curiosity to see and hear the young Pole, and when he arrived in Paris he created a sensation in society as well as in musical circles.

Besides his art young Chopin had the reputation of being an enthusiastic patriot. The revolution in Poland was just over; every one who came from that unhappy country seemed to have an air of romance about him, and the young musician, with his graceful beauty, his melancholy eyes and smile, playing as no Parisian had ever heard waltzes and polonaises played before, was naturally a strong attraction in the capital, and so he was soon established there, and gathered a wonderful circle of people about him. He knew all the famous men and women of the day. If some people found him cold and selfish, at least he seemed to have truly loved some of his chosen friends, and by many, both among his pupils and his friends, he was absolutely adored.

Unfortunately Chopin's health, never very strong, began to break soon after his twenty-fifth year. He went to Majorca to seek health, but returned to Paris only to break down again; and yet he had, like many people of his artistic nature, an energy and feverish activity which kept him up. So, in spite of remonstrances, he went to London, played there, and went constantly into society, burning out with a rush his feeble little lamp of life. He hastened back to his beloved Paris, where a favorite pupil, M. Gutman, had everything in readiness for him.

But Chopin's strength had entirely failed. He passed his days in weariness of mind and body, grateful for the loving attentions of friends, and particularly soothed by music. His pupil Gutman, his sister, and the Countess Potocka nursed him constantly, and they wheeled his piano to the bedroom door, where they could play and sing for him when he desired it. One evening about five o'clock he seemed dying, but suddenly he opened his eyes, and looking at Countess Potocka, murmured, "Sing."

She was weeping bitterly, but she went to the piano, and there sang the canticle to the Virgin, that wonderful song which Haweis tells us once saved the life of Stradella.

These were among the last sounds that reached the musician's ears. He died the peaceful death so often accorded to those who have suffered much with his disease, and while he lay in his last sleep friends came, filling all the room with flowers. Every one knew of his passionate love of them, and so, late roses and early autumn blossoms, and even spring violets and pansies, were strewn about him, until he seemed, they say, to be resting in some strangely sweet garden of God.

Chopin's great art was in his *harmonic progressions*, a term better to be understood after some study of thorough-bass, though even without this some idea of the meaning may be obtained and improved upon by studying different parts of different works.

A progression in harmony is, strictly speaking, the following up of one chord into another. An excellent idea is that chords should not be regarded only horizontally, as we are accustomed to think of them before us on the printed page, but as well *vertically*, which suggests to our mind their movement or *on-going* from one to the other. A chord is the combination of any tones, and the simplest chord of all is formed by adding to the tone its third and then its fifth, which is known as the triad symphone or concord from which all other chords are formed. The principal chords in the scale are known as the tonic, the dominant, and the sub-dominant, because their first notes are taken from the tonic,

SCHUBERT SEARCHING FOR THE ARTICLES HIS FELLOW-STUDENTS HAVE HIDDEN.

dominant, and sub-dominant of the scale. A number of changes, inversions, etc., belong to the arrangement of chords; and as progression depends so much upon them, their careful study should be regarded by any student as a most important branch of his or her work in music. What endless beauties may be wrought in progressions Chopin's music shows in perfection.

In Chopin's impromptus his peculiar power is most evident. An impromptu is a piece written down, yet in the style of extempore playing, or improvisation. Many musicians have been noted for their fine ideas in extempore playing. This is, to take up some musical idea, sit down, and at the piano elaborate it just as the ideas came. In impromptus the musician gives the idea that he is doing likewise, and the result in the music of Chopin and Schubert is something very fascinating. It may be as well to say that Beethoven and Mendelssohn never used this term for any of their music, but Chopin seems to have created it as something too dignified not to take a first place among musical significations. When you can play with ease Chopin's impromptu in C-sharp minor, or his impromptu Opus 36 (Opus stands for work), then you may feel that the drudgery of finger exercise is at an end, though its practice should be perpetual.

Schubert, the second in the trio I have mentioned, was

born in 1797, and was the youngest son of a family of eighteen, and from earliest childhood showed a passion for music: melody seeming to come as natural to him as the very air he breathed. At thirteen, overtures, quartets, symphonies, all sorts of compositions, were pouring forth from the young musician's brain and fingers, no sort of hardship daunting him, poverty and a rather rude home-life offering no obstacles whatever to his work. In 1816 Schubert was engaged in teaching little boys in his father's school, an occupation which seems to have afforded him no particular annoyance, probably because he worked at it mechanically, allowing his brain to employ itself as it would with musical composition while he listened to the *a-b ab* and the multiplication table of his little pupils. Having escaped one afternoon somewhat earlier than usual from his work, he shut himself up in a little room, the only spot belonging entirely to himself in his father's house. He had obtained possession of a volume of Goethe's poems, and sitting there he read the "Erl-king." Something seemed to fill his heart and mind and very soul as he read. It was an hour of tremendous inspiration; the words seemed to him to go to an accompaniment of rushing wind and of a fantastic melody; the forest stretched before him—the father and child riding on seemed to him to move to harmonies which he could not restrain himself from uttering; and then and there he seized his pen and wrote out the song which will be forever famous, never afterwards having to correct a single line of it, and occupying only as much time in the performance of this remarkable work as it took to actually write the notes down upon the paper. If Schubert had never written another line, his fame might well rest upon this composition. Every great singer, every great pianist has undertaken an interpretation of it; thousands have been realized by the publishers of it, and in the lives of various people we read of the effect produced by it upon their minds at different important periods; as, for instance, when Jean Paul Richter, the poet, dying and blind, desired, a few hours before his death, to hear it sung for the last time; and we have also a picture of Goethe, aged, and living much in the past, begging of Madame Devrient to sing it once more for him.

Schubert, warm-hearted, although at times intensely melancholy, had a charmed circle of friends; but he was not always a good companion, his natural inclination to depression depriving him of that element of *bonhomie* which is necessary in order to be always *en rapport* with one's gay companions. He was plain in appearance, not strong, although rather large, and walked with a stoop which made him awkward; but he was capable of all the suffering which comes from a sensitive and nervous temperament, and he had trouble enough to excuse many of his morbid feelings.

Beethoven, during his last illness, learned to appreciate the younger composer, and between the periods of his great suffering he spent much time poring over Schubert's music; and almost in his last moments the eyes of the great master rested upon his friend, and it is said that he strove vainly over and again to say something to him as he held his hand in a last farewell. In keeping with a German fashion, Schubert and some of his friends, on the day of Beethoven's funeral, drank to the soul of the great man. Some one suggested to drink to the one who should go next, whereupon Schubert started up, and filling a glass, turned aside, drinking to himself.

It is not possible to give you here a full account of his various symphonies, quartets, masses, quintets, sonatas, and songs; the last great work was completed in 1828. This was the seventh symphony in C, and it was performed to a crowded and enthusiastic audience. Fame and worldly success were just reaching forth their hands to lead him to the heights of peaceful content, but his health completely failed. In November, 1828, he expired at the age of thirty-one.

At Leipsic the news of Schubert's death reached painfully a young man who had been his devoted admirer since boyhood. This was Robert Schumann, then a lad of eighteen, working hard, composing, and building the foundation for a great musical career. Schumann's first strong impetus towards a musical life was when, at nine years of age, he made a journey to Carlsbad with a relative to hear Moscheles play, and the influence of this master's technique never left him. His father was a bookseller at Zwickau, in Saxony, and although he knew little of music, interested himself strongly in his son's talent, and at the same time gave him an excellent education. After leaving the University of Leipsic he travelled, making the acquaintance of various famous people and absorbing much material which he was later to turn to excellent account in his musical compositions. To follow Schumann's life would be highly interesting to the student of his work, since in it we find so many evidences of what influenced his compositions. The story for many years is a highly interesting one, including the events which led to his marriage with the gifted daughter of the old musician known as Papa Wieck.

The first performance of one of Schumann's symphonies took place at Zwickau in 1832, and Clara Wieck, then a girl of thirteen, was the pianist. Schumann, as well as all who heard her, was filled with enthusiasm, and from that moment seems to have adored the child who was later to become his wife. He had not poverty to contend with, and was therefore able to indulge many of his fancies in a musical career, and also to become interested in the publication of a musical paper. He associated himself with all the leading musicians and authors of the day, and on his marriage, in 1840, life seemed to begin with every promise of human happiness. Both husband and wife shared simple domestic tastes, and at the same time were heart and soul musicians. Clara Schumann* was the leading pianist of Germany, and he was one of its first composers. Their home at Leipsic formed a noted centre for everything that was delightful artistically, but both husband and wife enjoyed periods of seclusion and study. The intimacies of the Schumanns with Mendelssohn, Brahms, Joachim, and others are almost famous, so inspiring and devoted were they; but in spite of all that was so attractive in home and artistic life, Schumann's health failed: the natural tendency towards the morbid, which had always been a strong element in his nature, increased, and the last years of his life were passed in a private asylum near Bonn. His insanity took the form of melancholia. Naturally his musical work impressed him strongly, and various themes haunted him, so that he was driven to the verge of despair in trying to work them out. The very last came with the consolation of a more peaceful period, and in the arms of his wife, July 29, 1856, he passed quietly away.

---

* Madame Schumann still continues to delight the most cultured audiences (1886).

MADAME CLARA SCHUMANN.

CHAPTER XVIII.

Musical Culture.—A Young Girl's Diary.—Stepping-stones.—An Over-romantic Student.

ONE day a group of girls in a foreign conservatory sat down to discuss what music they liked best. With one exception, all were Americans, who had recently entered the B—— Conservatory. The preference was for operatic music; with some for Beethoven, and others for Mendelssohn.

Their musical education had been of the ordinary sort. They had studied compositions which were selected with no view to progress, and with no systematic idea of the right sort of cultivation, yet all were tolerably good performers; that is, their facility had justified them in going abroad to study in a regular musical school, and, like most American students, they had quick minds, a genuine musical enthusiasm—not the sort of patience or diligence which marks the German student, not the brilliancy of the French girl, who learns to make use of her fingers with marvellous rapidity, but their appreciations were ready to be cultivated, and their kind of enthusiasm was wholesome.

A year later any one of the group would have been surprised had she been reminded of the opinions expressed by her that day. System had stepped in with the slow but sure culture of a whole year's hearing of only the very best music. If you were studying astronomy or chemistry, would it occur to you that you could by any chance profit by mixing up all the chapters in your text-books, taking up any part at any time, and giving the end the first place in your mind? I am sure such a plan would seem absurd in the extreme; yet so few young people studying music stop to consider the necessity of avoiding just such a ridiculous jumble, that in this chapter I want to talk about certain arrangements for musical practice which I have seen work very well.

To begin with, remember that every moment you can give to your piano is valuable if used in the right way—five minutes at a time is profitable; on the other hand, every moment wasted in stupid or careless playing is a direct injury. Of course, even in our severest studies we like to be amused, and one always can be amused at the piano, except when one is playing finger exercises, over which you can at least be interested.

A very entertaining thing is to have a musical diary, in which one records each day what was practised or learned, with comments on the composer's style, any peculiar formation of chords or arrangement of notes, and any portions which have seemed most difficult. You have no idea, until you make the experiment, how such a book marks one's progress, and how interesting it becomes to look back upon. Reading such an one the other day, I was amused and interested in noting how difficulties which in January seemed insurmountable had vanished by May. This book was kept with alternate leaves of music-paper carefully inserted, so that the owner, who was certainly an anxious, if not a brilliant student, could put down or make note of anything which occurred to her as she wrote, and sometimes the result was very interesting and entertaining. At the end of each month the results were summed up with a note of what had been accomplished. Perhaps a few pages from such a diary will serve to illustrate my idea:

"*January 3d.*—Practised one hour to-day on Czerny's studies, and half an hour's Plaidy, the old five fingers. I then tried Mozart's minuet in E-flat major, hoping to make the staccato parts less heavy. After playing it a few times, I hunted out some bits of my exercises with special reference to those pieces, and after ten minutes found I could go back to the minuet much better. Read four pages of Haydn.

"*January 4th.*—Usual exercises practised, the minuet and Schumann's 'Slumber Song.' Noticed the peculiarities of some of the bars, and how very necessary it is to make the left-hand work smoothly. Worked ten minutes extra on left-hand finger exercises. Found it rather hard work. Went to one of Von Bülow's concerts in the evening, and returned wondering if I could ever accomplish anything. Was delighted to hear that he practised finger exercises an hour a day. He played Beethoven's 'Sonata Appasionata,' and fairly *rushed* it. I heard that Beethoven composed that sonata during a terrible thunder-storm, and Mr. —— says no one can play it like Liszt, and that when Rubinstein plays it he is apt to alter little bits here and there just to suit his mood. When I heard Madame Essipoff, she took a great deal of it very tenderly. Von Bülow is very effective, but certainly tremendous over it.

"*January 6th.*—Tried to read the 'Appasionata' with Mr. ——. Too much for me, but it gave me an idea of the majesty of the whole thing. In practising Mendelssohn's 'Spring Song' to-day I suddenly discovered how to do the arpeggio in the bass, and worked simply at those portions without reference to the rest for a time. Mendelssohn wrote the 'Spring Song' for one of his sister's festive occasions. When Moscheles went for the first time after Mendelssohn's death to see his wife Cecile, he played the 'Spring Song' for her, and it brought back to them both all their tenderest memories, so that it must have been most dear to the composer.

"*January 8th.*—Miss H—— spent two hours here to-day, and played all sorts of things. She has just come home from four years' musical study abroad, chiefly in Dresden and Berlin. She showed me how Deppe teaches his pupils to hold the fingers—to curve the hand always slightly outward and sink the knuckle part a little. She did some exercises very well, but her manner was excessively languid. She does not seem to have much musical instinct, and so it seemed to me waste of time, unless, as Mr. —— says, she could devote herself to harmony, and so enjoy music as a science. I played two of Chopin's waltzes for her, and was very glad of the suggestions she offered me about my fingering, which it seems to me I ought to consider more than I do. She described Liszt's manner as very entertaining. He is never twice quite alike, she says—sometimes satirical, sometimes playful; but she says his playing can never be described. It is simply perfect, especially in all legato passages. She used to see Tausig very often, and said that except Liszt he was the most wonderful pianist she had ever heard—but such an eccentric creature! like some half-human thing, quite elfish. He died very young, and was a great loss to the musical world.

"*February 1st.*—In my musical note-book to-day I took for an example in modulation the 'Largo Appasionata' from Beethoven's Sonata, Opus No. 2. The original key is D and it works readily into the dominant, but goes from that into D minor. For a sudden transition it is remarkably beautiful, and the manner in which it works back to D is highly interesting."

These quotations from a young girl's diary, which, as you see, was concerned only with musical matters, will perhaps show you what might be done in this way; and I am very sure such a book would add greatly to the interest of musical study. Various anecdotes of different compositions are included, as, for example—

"*February* 10*th.*—I played Schubert's 'Serenade' to-day, with G—— doing the violin obligato delightfully. He told me that Schubert had composed this charming work, with its suggestions of moonlight and rose-scented gardens, in the midst of the din and racket of a carousal from which he escaped, leaving his companions over their beer and songs at one end of the restaurant, while at the other, in an open window, he sat jotting down notes for this exquisite song."

And again:

"When Mendelssohn was composing the 'Elijah' he was in doubt about one passage, and accordingly he went to an intimate friend who was likewise a good critic, and played it over for him without saying whose or what it was. When he had finished, Mendelssohn calmly inquired, 'What do you think of that? at least, what would be your opinion of a work in which that could be included?'

"'That it ought to make the composer famous,' was the answer, whereupon Mendelssohn said nothing and went his way; but so strong was the impression made upon his impromptu critic's mind, that he declared that to him the whole of the 'Elijah,' when he heard it later and recognized this portion, seemed to be concentrated in that one particular portion, or to radiate therefrom."

From one of the monthly "summings up" I will quote a passage:

"*May* 31*st*.—This month I feel I have accomplished very little in the way of expression, but a great deal in overcoming certain difficulties. I really can play the E minor scale fairly well, and the 'Moonlight Sonata' no longer stares me in the face as something which I am never to execute. I have made, this month, a careful study of musical terms, writing them all down with definitions."

At the end of the year the diarist has put down a list of what she had learned and what concerts she had attended, and in a little companion volume the programmes of the concerts, with photographs of the performers.

There was no special literary merit in that little book, but I can safely say it carried the writer over tall places, and now suggests many an hour of work made fascinating instead of prosaic. The romantic element in musical study can be carried to a very ridiculous extreme, yet it may safely be allowed to tinge one's labors; for no art possesses such a field for poetic aspirations.

I would not for worlds suggest to my young readers to follow the example of a young person of twelve whom I once knew, and who went through a whole year of very commonplace musical study—in which, I am sorry to say, she accomplished but little—pretending to herself she was in Vienna studying at a conservatory, the *protégée* of a famous master, giving concerts and being treated as a prodigy. Little Miss K——, who, as you see, had a most vivid imagination, used to take her lessons with her little head just full of these fancied scenes, and on leaving her teacher's house would walk home with a servant, still assuming to herself that she was in Vienna, the observed of all observers. No profit came of all this to her playing, as you may easily believe, for in her case the ardor all went to the imaginary side, and the necessity of real work did not occur to her. It is well for young students to feel the poetry and loftiness of the art they are pursuing, but they should at the same time avoid eccentric vagaries.

CHAPTER XIX.

The Purpose of the Book.—Technique.—Standard Authorities.—Professional Pianists.—Books on Music.—Conservatories at Home and Abroad.—The Expense of Foreign Study.—Shining Lights.—Authorities used.—How to study Music profitably.

DURING the appearance of a portion of this little work in HARPER's YOUNG PEOPLE, a great many questions have been written me in regard to methods of study, instruction, and technique, and it seems advisable to address a final chapter to all such friendly inquirers, as well as to any readers who might be interested on the same points. To all such let me in the commencement say that I have neither the ability nor the desire to do more than make general helpful suggestions through this book; that methods of piano practice are too various to classify; that good instruction is the only kind worth having, and, fortunately, may be had in almost every city in America to-day, while foreign masters have learned to regard us as a tuneful and decidedly music-loving nation, according a special welcome to American students.

Technique is the foundation of art, and the study of harmony, guided by professors and writers like Cornell, Parker, Richter, and various other standard authorities, has advanced to a position wherein it is considered as part of the general culture as well as art of the day. Professional pianists are so numerous that the best of music may be heard on all sides, and this is certainly the most useful sort of stimulus to the young student. Books on music, technical, biographical, and discursive, are to be had by writers whose professional standing warrants their most dogmatic utterances.

In America conservatories of music have been started in all the principal cities, and in many instances are well managed and conducted. Abroad, the schools of Leipsic, Berlin, Paris, Stuttgart, etc., rank highly on the Continent, while in London two academies give a fine course of musical study and possess various scholarships. To give an estimate of the expense of musical study abroad, as I have been constantly asked to do, is a difficult matter, since so much depends upon the place of study chosen and the methods pursued, but I think that any prudently inclined student might be safe to venture abroad for musical education on an income of five hundred dollars a year, while I have known of its being done on even less.

Fifty years ago the number of professional pianists was so small that an amateur rarely had an opportunity for hearing good music or the least incentive for study from prominent examples. At the present day, while Liszt, Rubenstein, and Von Bulow head the list, a host of shining lights follow in their train, and the world seems full of the harmonious echoes they have wakened into life. It is scarcely possible to mention these artists all by name, but among prominent women of the day, all of whom I take for granted are willing to recognize Madame Clara Schumann as the leader of their sex in her art, we may pay this brief homage to Madame Essipoff, Madame Helen Hopekirk, Mademoiselle Janotha, and Madame Madeleine Schiller. So many new stars are constantly appearing, that before these words are printed it may be that other names will seem to belong to the record of famous *pianistes* of the day.

I trust that it will be seen by all my readers that no advice is offered in this little volume as from a professional musician, and that no suggestions contained within its pages are intended to do more than stimulate the ardor of the student who is working under good instruction.

All authorities consulted have been the best; all those quoted have been long recognized as governing musical decisions. The various methods for study suggested are the result of practical experience, and incidents relating to living persons or their friends have come from the most direct source. Personal sentiments which are only matters of taste need not have any special weight with the reader whose experience in musical life inclines him to an opposite opinion, since, fortunately, the world of art is large and fertile enough to include every variety of individuality. The technical portions of the book, as may readily be seen, are introduced only to illustrate or explain the form of composition especially under consideration, or to rouse an interest in the real study of harmony; while it is to be hoped that the lives of the great masters—the classicists—will give to piano study the touch of inspiration which comes from the story of those who have caused the divine art to unfold and reveal its treasures—to open wide its portals to those who knock with the password of interpretation ready on their lips.

Music must be loved to be studied profitably, but even then it reaches the depths of the heart and soul by a process of absorption which culture certainly develops. Each new step taken in the right direction widens the horizon and suggests new possibilities for the loving student, and it is an art which to such an one can never be thankless while the heart beats or the ears are not deaf to sound.

I can hardly do better than to bid my young readers farewell with an extract from Haweis's "Book on Musical Memories," in which he speaks of the power of music over mind and body:

"Music is not only a body healer, it is a mind regulator.

The great educational function of music remains almost to be discovered. The future mission of music for the million is the Discipline of Emotion. * * * Music rouses the emotions. Inward activities, long dormant or never before awakened, are called up, and become new powers within the breast; for, remember, emotion nerves for action. The stupidest horse that goes up hill to the sound of bells, the timidest soldier that marches to battle with fife and drum, the most delicate girl who spins round tireless in the dance, the poorest laborer who sings at his work—any of them is good enough to prove that music rouses and sustains emotion. * * * Music disciplines and controls emotion. That is the explanation of the art of music, as distinguished from the mere power of the musical sound. You can rouse with a stroke; but to guide, to moderate, to control, to raise and depress, to combine, to work out a definite scheme involving appropriate relations and proportions of force, and various mobility—for this you require the subtle machinery of an art; and the direct machinery for stirring up and regulating emotion is the wonderful vibratory mechanism created by the art of music."

INDEX.

A.

"A Calm Sea and a Prosperous Voyage," 186.
"A staid musicke ordered for grave dancing," 131.
Accent, 71.
Accidentals, 77, 78.
Acute sounds, 39.
Adagio, 121.
Adagio, largo, 129.
Adagio time, 162.
"Adelaide," 169.
"Agamemnon," 95.
Agnus Dei, 162.
Agreeable concords, 110.
Allegorical subjects, 186.
Allegorical performance, 62.
Allegro, 121, 128, 129.
"Allegro moderato," 129.
Allegro themes, 129.
Allemandes, 132.
Amateur, 18, 232.
Ambrose, St., 152.
"Amen," 93.
America, 63.
American students, 231.
Ancient Canto Fermo, 161.
Andante, 121, 128, 129.
Answer, 61.
Apostle of the Apocalypse, 159.
"Appasionata," 226.
Arias, 91.
Arpeggio, 50.
Arrangements, 112.
Arrangement of notes, 225.
Astronomy, 224.
Augmented interval, 48.
Augmented second, 76.
Avolio, Mrs., 88.

B.

Bach, Ambrosius, 53.
Bach, John Sebastian, 13, 43, 44, 53, 55–57, 59, 60, 62, 66, 67, 109, 140, 188, 190, 191, 202.
Bach's gavottes, 113.
Ballads, 111.
"Ballet Comique de la Royne," 190.
Band, 189.
Bardi, Giovanni, Conte di Vernio, 94.
Bar line, 70.
Bars, 58, 59, 69, 225.
Bartholdy, Felix Mendelssohn, 188, 197.
Basis of theory, 56.
Basque race, 62.

Bass, 191.
Bass drum, 193.
Bassoon, 168, 193.
Bass trumpet, 193.
Bayreuth festival, 96.
Beat, 71.
Beethoven, Jean, 165.
Beethoven, Ludwig von, 21, 22, 26, 111, 128, 161, 162, 165–167, 175, 202, 208, 220, 223.
Beethoven's andantes, 113.
Berlin, 64, 65, 197, 232.
Bible, 62, 65.
Biblical scenes, 62.
Big drum, 111.
"Big noises," 111.
Binchoys, 154.
Bishop, Sir Henry, 194.
Bodleian library, 40.
"Book on Musical Memories," 234.
Brahms, 175.
Branles, 131.
Breve, 41.
British Museum, 98.
Britton, Thomas, 87.
Broader harmony, 150.
Bulow, Von, 30, 33, 233.
Buononcini, 83.
Byron, John, 83, 87.

C.

Caccini, 95.
Cadences, 123.
Cadenzas, 175.
Canon imitation, 60.
Cantabile, 92.
Cantata, 124, 126.
Canticle, 213.
Canto Fermo, 154.
Canzonettes, 96, 97.
Cardinal Pisani, 159.
Catches, 103.
Cathedral at Winchester, 40.
Cavaliere, Emilio del, 91.
Chaconne, 59, 132.
Chamber music, 106, 193.
Chamber organ, 87.
Chant, 44.
Chapel, 161.
Chapel-master, 155.
Chapel of St. Maria Maggiore, 156.
Chapel organ, 85.
Château de Moutiers, 190, 191.
Chelsea, 104, 140.
Cherubini, 161.
Chitarone, 98.
Chopin, François, 27, 212, 217, 227.
Choral writing, 92.
Chorales, 63.
Chord, 74.
Chorda, 14, 18.
Chords, 74, 214, 217.
Choristers, 63.
Chorus, 90.
Christian plays, 63.
Christoph, Johann, 53.
Chromatic alteration, 76.
Church music, 124, 149.
Church of St. John in Rome, 100.
Cibber, Colley, 87.
Cibber, Mrs., 88.
Citherns, 28.
Citoles, 28.
Civilization, 53.
Clarionet, 193.
Classical, 112.
Classicists, 234.
Clavi, 14.

Index.

Clavichord, 14, 15, 56.
Clavicytheriums, 28.
Clerkenwell Green, 87.
Closer time, 61.
Club of minstrels, 119.
Code, 61.
Codetta, 61.
Colonia, Franco de, 41.
"Comfort ye my people," 93.
Common time, 58.
Composer, 53.
Composers' licences, 129.
Compositions, 119.
Con brio, 129.
Concert in Hicksford's Rooms, 134.
Concert-room, 172.
Concertos, Liszt's, 176.
Concertos, movements of, 175.
Concertos, Mozart's, 174.
Concerts, 173, 174.
Concerts in Paris, 175.
Concord, 214.
Contra bass tuba, 193.
Contrapuntal skill, 59.
Corelli, 125, 126, 127.
Cornell, 231.
Cornets, 189.
Corno di bassetto, 193.
Corsi, 96, 98.
Council of Trent, 156.
Counterpoint, 32, 56, 61, 98, 109.
Counter-subject, 61.
Courantes, 132.
Covent Garden, 90.
Credo, 161, 162.
Cristofari, 20.
Curtz, 119, 120.
Cymbals, 111, 193.
Czerny, 225.

D.

"Dafne," 97.
"Dash," 113.
"Dance therewith tunefully and harmoniously," 189.
Dauphine, 57.
Dauphiness, 106.
Dead march, 87.
Degrees, 48.
Deppe, 227.
"Der Freischütz," 182, 184, 186.
Descent of scale, 75.
Devrient, Madame, 219.
Devrient, Edward, 65, 66, 68, 208, 219.
"Dido and Æneas," 104.
Diminished interval, 48, 51, 52.
Diminished seventh, 52.
Discipline of emotions, 235.
Dominant, 61, 72, 74, 128, 228.
Dominant chord, 214.
Dominant relative major, 174.
Dominant seventh, 175.
"Don Giovanni," 26, 130.
"Don't make a cadenza, but go on at once to the following," 175.
Dot, 72.
Double basses, 193.
Double bassoon, 193.
Dramatic, 62.
Dresden, 227.
"Dressed quickly," 145.
Drums, 189.
Drury Lane, 80.
Dryden, 104.
Dubourg, Mr., 88.
Ducal chapel at Stella, 55.
Duc de Joyeuse, 189, 190.
Duchess of Queensbury, 87.
"Duets for four hands," 141.

Du Fay, 154.
Duke of Saxe, 84.
Dulcimers, 28.
Durante, 160, 161.

E.

Early Christian music, 33.
Early Church, 63.
Early melodic form, 163.
Easter-time, 157.
Ecclesiastical schools, 153.
"Echo et Narcisse," 112.
"Effects," 192.
Egyptians, 112.
Eighteenth century, 53.
Elector of Cologne, 165.
Elements of true musical inspiration, 112.
"Elijah," 204, 206, 208, 228, 229.
Elizabeth, Queen, 16, 131.
England, 40.
English musician, 70.
Episcopal Church of England, 153.
Episode, 61.
"Erl-king," 218.
Essipoff, Madame, 226, 233.
Esterhazy, Prince, 120.
Ethelred II., 40.
Europe, 190.
"Euryanthe," 184.
"Eurydice," 43.
Eutin, 178.
Execution, 56.
Extempore playing, 217.

F.

F note, 39.
"Family of tones," 72.

"Fance," 201.
"Faust," 42, 201.
Few rules for composition, 58.
"Fidelio," 186.
"Field-and-flower," 141.
Finish of melody, 73.
First symphony of Haydn's, 120.
Flanders, 40.
Florence, 94.
Flutes, 189.
"Following the marks," 72.
"For benefit of Miss Mozart and Master Mozart," 134.
Founder of opera in classical form, 106.
Founder of symphony, 121.
Four-line stave, 41.
Four movements of sonata, 128.
Four movements of symphony, 121.
Four perfect intervals, 49.
Fourteenth century, 91, 152.
Fourth century, 63.
Fractions of a bar, 72.
France, 121, 132.
Franck, Herr, 114.
Frege, Frau, 207.
Frescobaldi, 59.
Fugue, 62, 163.
Fugue in minor, 61.
Fugue of Bach, 74.
Funeral cantata, 166.
Fusignano, 126.

G.

Galileo Vincent, 96.
Gallards, 131.
Gavottes, 56–59, 62.
Genius, 55.

Index.

Genoa, 100.
George I., 79.
George II., 109.
Germany, 79.
"Glasses," 110.
Glees, 103.
Gluck, 105, 106, 109–112.
"Go," 113.
Goethe, 201, 202, 204.
Good-breeding in music, 72.
Good-Friday, 90.
Gospel choruses, 63.
Gounod, 161.
Gradual progressions, 44.
Grand fugues, 60.
Grave sounds, 139.
Greater intervals, 50.
Greek lyrical dramas, 95.
Greeks, 97.
Gregory, St., 33, 44, 152, 153.
Guicciardi, Countess, 169.
Gutman, M., 213.

H.

Half-bar, 59.
Half-steps, 49, 50, 52, 57, 72, 75.
Halle, 84.
Hamburg, 55, 114.
Handel, 59, 79, 80, 83–85, 87, 88, 109, 127, 185, 192, 195.
Hanoverian court, 79.
Harmonica, 110.
Harmonic changes, 60.
Harmonic forms, 51.
Harmonic progressions, 214.
Harmony, 32, 43, 44, 46, 56, 59, 112.
Harmony class, 33.
Harps, 20, 114, 193.
Harpsichord, 18, 19, 86, 106, 119, 140.

Haweis, 213, 234.
Haydn, 13, 25, 117, 119, 120–123, 129, 167, 225.
"Hebrides," 186.
Henry IV. of France, 98.
Henry VII., 14.
Hiller, 197, 206.
Historical oratorios, 91.
Holland, 166.
Holyshead, 88.
Homophonic, 97.
Hopekirk, Helen, Madame, 233.
Hucbaldus, 40.
Hummell, 203.
Humphries, 103.
Hunsden, Lord, 16.
Hymns, 103.

I.

"Ich lasse das mädchen das nicht will," 147.
"Il carno Sassone," 86.
"Il Parnasso," 111.
Imperfect fifth, 49.
Improvising, 60.
Interval, 48, 76.
Interval, imperfect, 48.
Interval of diminished seventh, 61, 72.
Introduction, 187.
Instruction, 231.
"Introit," 162.
"Invitation to the waltz," 182.
"Israel in Egypt," 87.
"It comes from thence," 122.
Italian C, 58.
Italian masters, 162.
Italian opera, 98.

Italian opera music, 80.
Italy, 86, 132.

J.

Janotha, Mademoiselle, 521.
"Jephthah," 89.
Joachim, 207, 222.
Jesuit College at Kommotau, 106.
"Joshua," 89.
"Judas Maccabæus," 89, 92.

K.

Kapellmeister, 203.
Keller, 114.
Keller, Ann, 119.
Key, 72.
Key-notes, 72, 73, 128.
"Key of C," 73.
Key-tone, 73, 75.
King of Wurtemburg, 181.

L.

Lacrimoso, 140.
"L' Amfi parnasso," 95.
Landmarks, 44.
"La Ressurezione," 91.
"Lascia ch' io Pianga," 80.
Latin fugare, 57.
Lawes, Henry, 70.
Leading note, 73.
Leading principles, 73.
Leger lines, 40.
Leipsic, 206, 220, 232.
Lesser third, 50.
"Let there be light," 122.
Libretto, 98, 120.
Lichnowsky, Princess, 25.

Limitations, 56.
Liszt, 33, 233.
Literature, 64.
Louis XIII., 99.
Louis's court, 57.
Lulli, 99.
Lutes, 28.
Lyres, 28, 95.
Lyric drama, 111.

M.

Madrigals, 14, 59, 97, 104, 125.
Magnificats, 159.
Main rules for the fugue, 62.
Major interval, 48–50.
Major key, 59, 73, 87.
Major scale, 48.
Major second, 50, 51.
Major seventh, 75.
Mantua, 95.
Manuscript page, 54.
Maria de Medici, 98.
Marie Antoinette, 105, 111
Marius, 20.
Mass, 43, 118.
Masses of notes, 71.
Mass in B minor, 160.
Mass, Marcelli, 148.
Mass, requiem, 148, 158.
Masterly manner, 57.
Material of a key, 73, 74.
Measure, 7.
Mediæval, 91.
Melodic form, 155.
Melodious forms, 100.
Melody, 41, 44, 152, 156.
Melody chant, 154.
Melvil, Sir James, 16.

Index. 243

Mendelssohn, Fanny, 204.
Mendelssohn, Felix, 27, 28, 64, 68, 113, 144, 175, 195, 196, 200–208.
Mendelssohn, Madame, 67, 226.
Messiah, 78, 79, 88, 89, 92.
Method, 112.
Metre, 70.
Metre of music, 70.
Middle ages, 90.
Middle C, 48–50.
Milan, 109.
Milton, 104.
Minor cadences, 93.
Minor interval, 48, 50.
Minor key, 59, 73.
Minor scale, 75.
Minor scale of E, 30.
Minor seventh, 52.
Minor sixth, 76.
Minor third, 75.
Minuet, 121, 128, 130.
Moderately quick, 72.
Molto, 129.
Monodia, 97.
Montpensier, Mademoiselle de, 99.
Moscheles, 27, 28, 202–208.
Mozart, 18, 25, 26, 111, 121, 129, 130, 134–149.
Musical academy, 65.
Musical diary, 45, 227–230.
Musical drama, 95.
Musical ideas, 71.
Musical notation, 51, 52.
Musical note-book, 52.
Musical taste, 72.
Musical terms, 44.
Musician, 53.
Music-book, 57, 62.
Music-loving nations, 55.

Music manuscript, 54.
Music masters, 114.
Music-room, 85.

N.

National hymn, 123.
Naturals, 77.
Neumæ, 39, 41.
Notation, 48.
Note, 44.
Note-book, 44.
"Notre cher Gluck," 111.

O.

Octave, 48.
Ohrdruff lyceum, 53.
Opera, 33, 43, 94, 96, 122.
Opera-house, 80.
Operetta, 104.
Operatic styles, 100.
Oratorio, 33, 43, 87–89, 122.
Orchestra, 33, 64, 95, 122.
Orchestral music, 106.
Organ, 56, 60, 83, 106, 119.
Organist, 53, 64.
Original key, 78.
"Orpheus and Eurydice," 111.
Overture, 96.

P.

"Papa Haydn," 121.
Parker, 48, 231.
Paris, 232.
Passacailles, 56, 59.
Passaglia, 59.
Passion music, 62, 63, 65.
Passion oratorios, 63.

Pathetic movement, 60.
Pathos, 121.
Pepusch, Dr., 87.
Perfect interval, 48, 49, 52.
Peri, 43, 96, 98.
Phrase, 44.
Pianist, 70.
Piano-forte, 13, 56.
"Pieces," 59.
Poetry, 60.
Polyphonic schools, 97.
Pope, 87.
Presto, 121, 128.
Primary accent, 72.
Prime, 49.
Progressions, 73, 74.
Psalteries, 28.
Purcell, Henry, 103–105.

Q.

Quarter note, 59.
Quartettes, 106.

R.

Ratio of sound, 49.
Recitative, 63.
Red line, 39.
Reformation, 63.
Reinkin, 55.
Related key, 74.
Relative major, 123.
Religious performance, 62.
Rest, 72.
Reuter, Herr, 117.
Rhythm, 69, 70, 72.
Rhythmical meaning, 71.
Richter, 219, 232.
Ries, 22.

Rinaccini, 98.
Rinaldo, 80, 86.
Romans, 97.
Rondo, 128.
Rubenstein, 33, 233.
Rules, 98.
Rules of harmony, 56, 99.

S.

Sacred and secular music, 109.
Sacred poems, 90.
Salzburg, 138.
"Samson," 89.
Sarabandes, 56, 59, 60, 132.
"Saul," 87.
Saxony, 84.
Scarlatti, 56, 86, 99, 100, 127, 160.
Scherzo, 121, 128, 130, 133.
Schiller, Madeleine, Madame, 233.
Schroter, 20.
Schubert, 129.
Schumann, Clara, Madame, 222, 233.
Score, 41, 42, 93.
Score of Messiah, 93.
Secondary accent, 72.
Second movement in sonatas, 128.
Semibreve, 41.
Semitone, 40.
Seven steps, 48.
Seventh century, 43, 60.
Shakespeare, 16.
Signature, 75.
Sistine chapel, 157.
Sixteenth century, 60.
Solo singers, 66.
Sonata, 77, 113, 119, 125, 126, 130, 132.
Sonata, perfection of the, 26.

Index.

Song, 44, 103.
Soprano, 118.
Sounds, 73.
South Kensington Museum, 98.
Spain, 62.
Spencer, 16.
Spinet, 18, 28, 84, 105.
Staff, 48.
Standard rules of art, 112.
Stave, 40, 69.
Steps, 52, 70.
Stradella, 100.
Stretto, 61.
Stuart, Mary, 16.
Study, 232.
Stuttgart, 232.
Suabia, 132.
Sub-dominant, 74.
Subject or motif, 60, 74, 112.
Suite, 125.
Swinging utterance, 71.
Symphony, 113, 128, 130.
Systematic grouping of notes, 70.

T.

T, 40.
"Tannhauser," 186.
"The Battle of Prague," 21, 31.
The family of notes, 46.
"The Harmonious Blacksmith," 87.
"The Magic Flute," 148.
Theme, 112.
"Theodora," 89.
The Passion music, 63.
"The Tempest," 104.
Thomas-Kirche, 60, 64.
Thomas-Schule, 60, 66.

Time, 161.
Torvelli, 173.
Trivirga, 38.
Twelve scales, 77.

U.

Unison, 49.
Unity of sound, 73.

V.

Varatanda, 60.
Vibrations, 49.
Vienna, 117, 119.
Violin, 53, 56, 119.
Virginal, 14, 15, 18, 28.
Vocal parts, 43.

W.

Wagner, 96, 186.
Walpole, Horace, 111.
Waltzes, 212.
Warsaw, 211.
Weber, Carl Maria von, 161, 162, 177-185, 208.
Weber family, 146-148.
Weimar, 202.
Werther, 20.
"We sat down in tears," 68.
Westminster Abbey, 103.
Whole steps, 50.
Wieck, Clara, 221.
Windsor, 80.
Words, 129.

Z.

Zelter, 66, 67.
Zither, 15.

THE END.

INTERESTING BOOKS FOR YOUNG PEOPLE.

Published by HARPER & BROTHERS.

☞ Harper & Brothers *will send their publications by mail, postage prepaid, to any part of the United States, Canada, or Mexico, on receipt of the price.*

THE WONDER CLOCK; or, Four-and-Twenty Marvellous Tales: Being One for each Hour of the Day. Written and Illustrated with 160 Drawings by Howard Pyle. Embellished with Verses by Katharine Pyle. Large 8vo, Ornamental Cloth, $3 00.

PEPPER AND SALT; or, Seasoning for Young Folks. Prepared and Profusely Illustrated by Howard Pyle. 4to, Illuminated Cloth, $2 00.

THOMAS W. KNOX'S WORKS. 8vo, Cloth. Profusely Illustrated.
    THE BOY TRAVELLERS IN MEXICO. $3 00.
    THE BOY TRAVELLERS IN AUSTRALASIA. $3 00.
    THE BOY TRAVELLERS ON THE CONGO. Adventures of Two Youths in a Journey with Henry M. Stanley "Through the Dark Continent." $3 00.
    THE BOY TRAVELLERS IN THE RUSSIAN EMPIRE. $3 00.
    THE BOY TRAVELLERS IN SOUTH AMERICA. A Journey through Ecuador, Peru, Bolivia, Brazil, Paraguay, Argentine Republic, and Chili. With Descriptions of Voyages upon the Amazon and La Plata Rivers. $3 00.
    THE VOYAGE OF THE "VIVIAN," to the North Pole and Beyond. Adventures of Two Youths in the Open Polar Sea. $2 50.
    THE BOY TRAVELLERS IN THE FAR EAST. Five Parts. $3 00 each. The Five Parts in a Box, $15 00.
        Part I. JAPAN AND CHINA.
        Part II. SIAM AND JAVA. With Descriptions of Cochin China, Cambodia, Sumatra, and the Malay Archipelago.
        Part III. CEYLON AND INDIA. With Descriptions of Borneo, the Philippine Islands, and Burmah.
        Part IV. EGYPT AND THE HOLY LAND.
        Part V. JOURNEY THROUGH AFRICA.
    HUNTING ADVENTURES ON LAND AND SEA. Two Parts. $2 50 each.
        Part I. THE YOUNG NIMRODS IN NORTH AMERICA.
        Part II. THE YOUNG NIMRODS AROUND THE WORLD.

CHARLES CARLETON COFFIN'S WORKS. Seven Volumes. Copiously Illustrated. Square 8vo, Cloth, $3 00 each.
    THE STORY OF LIBERTY.   THE BOYS OF '76.
    OLD TIMES IN THE COLONIES.   BUILDING THE NATION.
    DRUM-BEAT OF THE NATION.   MARCHING TO VICTORY.
        REDEEMING THE REPUBLIC.

Interesting Books for Young People.

INDIAN HISTORY FOR YOUNG FOLKS. By Francis S. Drake. Copiously Illustrated. 8vo, Cloth, $3 00.

HARPER'S YOUNG PEOPLE. Volumes IX. (1888) and VIII. (1887), 4to, Cloth, $3 50 each. (Volumes I., II., III., IV., V., VI., and VII., *out of print*.) Each Volume contains the Numbers for a year, with over 800 pages and about 700 Illustrations.

HARPER'S YOUNG PEOPLE SERIES. Ill'd. 16mo, Cloth, $1 00 per vol.

Toby Tyler; or, Ten Weeks with a Circus.—Mr. Stubbs's Brother (Sequel to "Toby Tyler").—Tim and Tip.—Raising the "Pearl."—Left Behind; or, Ten Days a Newsboy.—Silent Pete. By James Otis.

The Moral Pirates.—The Cruise of the "Ghost."—The Cruise of the Canoe Club.—The Adventures of Jimmy Brown.—A New Robinson Crusoe. By W. L. Alden.

Mildred's Bargain, and Other Stories.—Nan.—Rolf House.—Jo's Opportunity.—The Story of Music and Musicians.—The Colonel's Money.—The Household of Glen Holly. By Lucy C. Lillie.

Who was Paul Grayson? By John Habberton.

The Four Macnicols. By William Black.

The Talking Leaves: An Indian Story.—Two Arrows. A Story of Red and White. By W. O. Stoddard.

The Ice Queen. By Ernest Ingersoll.

The Lost City; or, The Boy Explorers in Central Asia.—Into Unknown Seas. By David Ker.

Prince Lazybones, and Other Stories. By Mrs. J. W. Hays.

Strange Stories from History for Young People. By G. Cary Eggleston.

Wakulla: A Story of Adventure in Florida.—The Flamingo Feather.—Derrick Sterling.—Crystal, Jack & Co. and Delta Bixby. By C. K. Munroe.

Uncle Peter's Trust. By Geo. B. Perry.

DIDDIE, DUMPS, AND TOT; OR, PLANTATION CHILD-LIFE. By Louise Clarke-Pyrnelle. Illustrated. 16mo, Cloth, $1 00.

NEW GAMES FOR PARLOR AND LAWN. By G. B. Bartlett. 16mo, Cloth, $1 00.

FROM THE FORECASTLE TO THE CABIN. By Capt. S. Samuels. Illustrated. 12mo, Extra Cloth, $1 50.

POLITICS FOR YOUNG AMERICANS. By Charles Nordhoff. 12mo, Half Leather, 75 cents; Paper, 40 cents.

GOD AND THE FUTURE LIFE. The Reasonableness of Christianity. By Charles Nordhoff. 16mo, Cloth, $1 00.

ANIMAL LIFE IN THE SEA AND ON THE LAND. A Zoology for Young People. By Sarah Cooper. Profusely Ill'd. 12mo, Cloth, $1 25.

THE BALL OF THE VEGETABLES, and Other Stories in Prose and Verse. By Margaret Eytinge. Illustrated. 8vo, Cloth, $2 00.

THE HISTORY OF A MOUNTAIN. By Élisée Reclus. Illustrated by L. Bennett. 12mo, Cloth, $1 25.

THE ADVENTURES OF A YOUNG NATURALIST. By Lucien Biart. With 117 Illustrations. 12mo, Cloth, $1 75.

AN INVOLUNTARY VOYAGE. By Lucien Biart. Illustrated. 12mo, Cloth, $1 25.

THE BOYHOOD OF MARTIN LUTHER. By Henry Mayhew. Illustrated. 16mo, Cloth, $1 25.

THE STORY OF THE PEASANT-BOY PHILOSOPHER. (Founded on the Early Life of Ferguson, the Shepherd-Boy Astronomer.) By Henry Mayhew. 16mo, Cloth, $1 25.

YOUNG BENJAMIN FRANKLIN. By Henry Mayhew. Illustrated. 16mo, Cloth, $1 25.

THE WONDERS OF SCIENCE; or, Young Humphry Davy. The Life of a Wonderful Boy. By Henry Mayhew. 16mo, Cloth, $1 25.

THE BOYHOOD OF GREAT MEN. By John G. Edgar. Illustrated. 16mo, Cloth, $1 00.

THE FOOTPRINTS OF FAMOUS MEN. By John G. Edgar. Illustrated. 16mo, Cloth, $1 00.

HISTORY FOR BOYS; or, Annals of the Nations of Modern Europe. By John G. Edgar. Illustrated. 16mo, Cloth, $1 00.

SEA-KINGS AND NAVAL HEROES. A Book for Boys. By John G. Edgar. Illustrated. 16mo, Cloth, $1 00.

THE WARS OF THE ROSES. By John G. Edgar. Illustrated. 16mo, Cloth, $1 00.

HOW TO GET STRONG, AND HOW TO STAY SO. By WILLIAM BLAIKIE. With Illustrations. 16mo, Cloth, $1 00; Paper, 50 cents.

SOUND BODIES FOR OUR BOYS AND GIRLS. By WILLIAM BLAIKIE. Illustrated. 16mo, Cloth, 40 cents.

DOGS AND THEIR DOINGS. By Rev. F. O. MORRIS, B.A. Illustrated. Square 8vo, Cloth, Gilt Sides, $1 75.

TALES FROM THE ODYSSEY FOR BOYS AND GIRLS. By C. M. B. 32mo, Paper, 25 cents; Cloth, 40 cents.

CAST UP BY THE SEA; or, The Adventures of Ned Gray. By Sir SAMUEL W. BAKER. Illustrated. 12mo, Cloth, $1 25; 4to, Paper, 15 cents.

THE ADVENTURES OF REUBEN DAVIDGER; Seventeen Years and Four Months Captive among the Dyaks of Borneo. By J. GREENWOOD. 8vo, Cloth, $1 25; 4to, Paper, 15 cents.

WILD SPORTS OF THE WORLD. A Book of Natural History and Adventure. By JAMES GREENWOOD. Illustrated. Crown 8vo, Cloth, $2 50.

HOMES WITHOUT HANDS: Being a Description of the Habitations of Animals. By the Rev. J. G. WOOD, M.A., F.L.S. With about 140 Illustrations. 8vo, Cloth, $4 50; Sheep, $5 00; Half Calf, $6 75.

THE ILLUSTRATED NATURAL HISTORY. By the Rev. J. G. WOOD. M.A., F.L.S. With 450 Engravings. 12mo, Cloth, $1 05.

CAMP LIFE IN THE WOODS; and the Tricks of Trapping and Trap Making. By W. HAMILTON GIBSON, Author of "Pastoral Days." Illustrated. 12mo, Cloth, $1 00.

NIMROD OF THE SEA; or, The American Whaleman. By WILLIAM M. DAVIS. With many Illustrations. 12mo, Cloth, $2 00.

ODD PEOPLE: Being a Popular Description of Singular Races of Man. By Captain MAYNE REID. With Illustrations. 16mo, Cloth, 75 cents.

Interesting Books for Young People. 5

COUNTRY COUSINS. Short Studies in the Natural History of the United States. By ERNEST INGERSOLL. Illustrated. 8vo, Cloth, $2 50.

FRIENDS WORTH KNOWING. Glimpses of American Natural History. By ERNEST INGERSOLL. Illustrated. 16mo, Cloth, $1 00.

PAUL B. DU CHAILLU'S WORKS ON AFRICA. Five Volumes. Illustrated. 12mo, Cloth, $1 50 each.
    THE COUNTRY OF THE DWARFS.   MY APINGI KINGDOM.
    WILD LIFE UNDER THE EQUATOR.   LOST IN THE JUNGLE.
    STORIES OF THE GORILLA COUNTRY.

ROUND THE WORLD; including a Residence in Victoria, and a Journey by Rail across North America. By a Boy. Edited by SAMUEL SMILES. Illustrated. 12mo, Cloth, $1 50.

THE SELF-HELP SERIES. By S. SMILES. 12mo, Cloth, $1 00 each.
    SELF-HELP.   CHARACTER.   THRIFT.   DUTY.

STORIES OF INVENTORS AND DISCOVERERS in Science and the Useful Arts. By JOHN TIMBS. Illustrated. 12mo, Cloth, $1 50.

OUR CHILDREN'S SONGS. Illustrated. 8vo, Cloth, $1 00.

FAMOUS LONDON MERCHANTS. A Book for Boys. By H. R. FOX BOURNE. Illustrated. 16mo, Cloth, $1 00.

PRAIRIE AND FOREST. A Description of the Game of North America, with Personal Adventures in their Pursuit. By PARKER GILLMORE. Illustrated. 12mo, Cloth, $1 50.

PUSS-CAT MEW, and Other New Fairy Stories for my Children. By E. H. KNATCHBULL-HUGESSEN. Illustrated. 12mo, Cloth, $1 25.

FAIRY TALES OF ALL NATIONS. By ÉDOUARD LABOULAYE. Translated by MARY L. BOOTH. Illustrated. 12mo, Cloth, Bevelled Edges, $2 00; Gilt Edges, $2 50.

LAST FAIRY TALES. By ÉDOUARD LABOULAYE. Translated by MARY L. BOOTH. Illustrated. 12mo, Cloth, Bevelled Edges, $2 00; Gilt Edges, $2 50.

Interesting Books for Young People.

THE THOUSAND AND ONE NIGHTS; or, The Arabian Nights' Entertainments. Translated and Arranged for Family Reading by E. W. LANE. 600 Illustrations. 2 vols., 12mo, Cloth, $3 50.

JACOB ABBOTT'S WORKS.

SCIENCE FOR THE YOUNG. Illustrated. 4 vols., 12mo, Cloth, $1 50 each.
- HEAT.
- LIGHT.
- WATER AND LAND.
- FORCE.

FRANCONIA STORIES. Illustrated. 16mo, Cloth, 75 cents each.
- MALLEVILLE.
- MARY BELL.
- ELLEN LINN.
- WALLACE.
- BEECHNUT.
- STUYVESANT.
- AGNES.
- MARY ERSKINE.
- RODOLPHUS.
- CAROLINE.

LITTLE LEARNER SERIES. Illustrated. 16mo, Cloth, 75 cents each.
- LEARNING TO TALK.
- LEARNING TO THINK.
- LEARNING ABOUT COMMON THINGS.
- LEARNING ABOUT RIGHT AND WRONG.
- LEARNING TO READ.

MARCO PAUL SERIES. Marco Paul's Voyages and Travels in the Pursuit of Knowledge. Illustrated. 16mo, Cloth, 75 cents each.
- IN NEW YORK.
- ON THE ERIE CANAL.
- IN THE FORESTS OF MAINE.
- IN VERMONT.
- IN BOSTON.
- AT THE SPRINGFIELD ARMORY.

RAINBOW AND LUCKY SERIES. Illustrated. 16mo, Cloth, 75 cents each.
- HANDIE.
- RAINBOW'S JOURNEY.
- THE THREE PINES.
- SELLING LUCKY.
- UP THE RIVER.

YOUNG CHRISTIAN SERIES. Illustrated. 12mo, Cloth, $1 75 each.
- THE YOUNG CHRISTIAN.
- THE CORNER STONE.
- THE WAY TO DO GOOD.
- HOARYHEAD AND M'DONNER.

THE YOUNG CHRISTIAN. A Memorial Volume. With a Sketch of the Author by one of his Sons. Steel-Plate Portrait of the Author, and Wood-cuts. 12mo, Cloth, $2 00.

Interesting Books for Young People.

ABBOTTS' (JACOB AND J. S. C.) BIOGRAPHICAL HISTORIES. Illustrated. 16mo, Cloth, $1 00 per volume.

CYRUS THE GREAT.	MARY QUEEN OF SCOTS.
DARIUS THE GREAT.	QUEEN ELIZABETH.
XERXES.	CHARLES I.
ALEXANDER THE GREAT.	CHARLES II.
ROMULUS.	HERNANDO CORTEZ.
HANNIBAL.	HENRY IV.
PYRRHUS.	LOUIS XIV.
JULIUS CÆSAR.	MARIA ANTOINETTE.
CLEOPATRA.	MADAME ROLAND.
NERO.	JOSEPHINE.
ALFRED THE GREAT.	JOSEPH BONAPARTE.
WILLIAM THE CONQUEROR.	HORTENSE.
RICHARD I.	LOUIS PHILIPPE.
RICHARD II.	GENGHIS KHAN.
RICHARD III.	KING PHILIP.
MARGARET OF ANJOU.	PETER THE GREAT.

THE HISTORY OF SANDFORD AND MERTON. By THOMAS DAY. 18mo, Half Bound, 75 cents.

JOHN BONNER'S CHILD'S HISTORIES.
    CHILD'S HISTORY OF GREECE. Illustrated. 2 vols., 16mo, Cloth, $2 50.
    CHILD'S HISTORY OF ROME. Illustrated. 2 vols., 16mo, Cloth, $2 50.
    CHILD'S HISTORY OF THE UNITED STATES. New Edition, Revised, and brought down to the Close of the Rebellion. Illustrated. 3 vols., 16mo, Cloth, $3 75.

THE STORY OF THE UNITED STATES NAVY, for Boys. By BENSON J. LOSSING. Illustrated. 12mo, Half Leather, $1 75.

FRENCH HISTORY FOR ENGLISH CHILDREN. By SARAH BROOK. With Illustrations and Colored Maps. 16mo, Cloth, $1 00.

CHILD'S HISTORY OF ENGLAND. By CHARLES DICKENS. Illustrated. 2 vols. in one, 16mo, Half Leather, 60 cents.

Interesting Books for Young People.

THE HISTORY OF A MOUTHFUL OF BREAD, and its Effect on the Organization of Men and Animals. By JEAN MACÉ. Translated by Mrs. ALFRED GATTY. 12mo, Cloth, $1 75.

THE SERVANTS OF THE STOMACH. By JEAN MACÉ. Reprinted from the London Edition, Revised and Corrected. 12mo, Cloth, $1 75.

HOME FAIRY TALES. By JEAN MACÉ. Illustrated. 12mo, Cloth, $1 75.

YOUTH'S HEALTH-BOOK. 32mo, Paper, 25 cents; Cloth, 40 cents.

STORIES OF THE OLD DOMINION. From the Settlement to the End of the Revolution. By JOHN ESTEN COOKE. Illustrated. 12mo, Cloth, $1 50.

FRED MARKHAM IN RUSSIA; or, The Boy Travellers in the Land of the Czar. By W. H. G. KINGSTON. Illustrated. Small 4to, Cloth, 75 cents.

SELF-MADE MEN. By CHARLES C. B. SEYMOUR. Many Portraits. 12mo, Cloth, $1 75.

ROBINSON CRUSOE, of York, Mariner; with a Biography of DEFOE. Illustrated. Complete Edition. 12mo, Cloth, $1 00.

THE SWISS FAMILY ROBINSON. Ill'd. 2 vols., 18mo, Cloth, $1 50.

THE SWISS FAMILY ROBINSON—Continued: being a Sequel to the Foregoing. 2 vols., 18mo, Cloth, $1 50.

THE PILGRIM'S PROGRESS. By JOHN BUNYAN. With a Life of the Author by ROBERT SOUTHEY. Illustrated. 12mo, Cloth, $1 00; Gilt Edges, $1 50.

THE CATSKILL FAIRIES. By VIRGINIA W. JOHNSON. Illustrated by ALFRED FREDERICKS. Square 8vo, Illuminated Cloth, $3 00.

WHAT MR. DARWIN SAW in his Voyage round the World in the Ship "Beagle." Illustrated. 8vo, Cloth, $3.00.

www.ingramcontent.com/pod-product-compliance
Lightning Source LLC
Chambersburg PA
CBHW032002230426
43672CB00010B/2241